IN SOLIDARITY, REV. JAMES FLYNN

by Marian T. Call

DORRANCE
PUBLISHING CO
EST. 1920
PITTSBURGH, PENNSYLVANIA 15238

Dorrance Publishing Co
585 Alpha Drive
Pittsburgh, PA 15238
Visit our website at *www.dorrancebookstore.com*

ISBN: 978-1-6442-6932-9
eISBN: 978-1-6442-6374-7

"The sleeping giant is one name for the public; when it wakes up, when *we* wake up, we are no longer only the public. We are civil society, the superpower whose non-violent means are sometimes for a shining moment, more powerful than violence, more powerful than regimes and armies. We write history with our feet and with our presence and our collective voice and vision."

Hope in the Dark
by Rebecca Solnit

CHAPTER 1

Jim Flynn standing in front of the I.C.E. Office in downtown Louisville.

In March of 2017, on a rainy Monday morning, a man stood alone outside the Immigration and Customs Enforcement Office in downtown Louisville holding a sign. Marnie McAllister, an editor for *The Record*, the Louisville Archdiocesan newspaper, describes the scene this way:

As it began to sprinkle on a cool morning in late March, Father James Flynn, a friend to immigrants around the Archdiocese of Louisville, stood in vigil in front of the Immigration and Customs Enforcement (I.C.E.) offices in downtown Louisville. He's been standing there, alone, a few days a week this Lenten season. He holds a sign that refers to the Gospel of Matthew, asking those who work for I.C.E., "I was a foreigner, and you?" This 87-year old priest said, in a statement submitted to *The Record*, that he stands in solidarity "with brothers and sisters of mine from other countries."

Fr. James Flynn's long-standing commitment to stand in solidarity with "brothers and sisters of mine from other countries" has recently been galvanized by President Donald Trump's harsh and punitive decision to follow through on a campaign promise he made to crack down on immigrants trying to enter the United States and to deport many who are already here. Because Jim has spent much of his life writing history with *his* feet and with *his* presence, he is not a man who will sit by and watch the resurgence of discrimination toward immigrants without acting. He said, "What's happening with the Trump Administration is that they are using what is called expedited deportations, which means that I.C.E officials can come and pick up almost any immigrants without a reason, suspending due process, even if they're ordinary citizens, with no criminal history. This is of great concern to many of us in the Solidarity Movement."

In July of 2017, Jim began meeting with a group of six other concerned members of Ascension Parish, who joined together to drink coffee (fair trade coffee, Jim points out) while they hashed over various actions they might take to address the immigration crisis. Their brainstorming birthed an idea of holding a vigil every Saturday on the corner of a busy street in Louisville, with the intersection of Breckinridge Lane and Hikes Lane being the first. Not long after this decision, word of their plans spread, and soon about 10 members of the Crescent Hill Presbyterian Church, who knew immigrants were being rounded up and arrested, began another vigil on Preston Highway. A third group from Epiphany Parish took their message to the corner of Shelbyville Road and Hurstbourne Lane. And yet a fourth group from St. William's Parish began a weekly vigil at the corner of Third Street and Cardinal Boulevard.

"Shortly a fifth group will gather to witness at Bardstown Road and Taylorsville

Road," Jim said. "We hold up a sign that says, **In Loving Memory of Those Who Have Been Deported by Immigration Authorities,** and below we list the first names of those who have been sent back to their countries of origin. We also hold up a larger sign, perhaps five feet by two feet, that says, **Immigrants and Refugees Welcome,** and we're distributing bumper stickers with the same sentiment."

Jim reports that as people drive by, some honk their horns in support for what they are standing for, while a few others express their disapproval. Those in favor outnumber the opponents by about 60 to one.

"We do get some negative responses," he said. "Occasionally, we'll receive rude gestures. One man who was stopped by a red light took the opportunity to inform me that he believes in immigration, but that people should do it 'the right way.' This indicates to me that he has little to no understanding of the context of why immigrants are here. A lot of Americans are convinced that they come to the United States to take our jobs, but they have no idea what they endure to get here or why they are fleeing their countries of birth. They are running away from destitution and civil unrest. The political, social, and economic factors have deteriorated to such an extent that people emigrate to try and find a better life. Dire poverty pulls them from Central America and Mexico in the hope they can find a job and send money back to help their families.

"People who roll down their car windows and speak to us about doing it the 'right way' have no idea of the grinding poverty many people from other countries face daily. During another of our vigils, a woman hung half of her body out of the car, and shouted, 'They don't pay taxes.'"

The original group's planned activities continued to gain momentum. When they could, several priests gathered with Jim at the corner of Bardstown Road and Goldsmith Lane each Thursday of the month from 4:30-5:30 PM.

In addition to these vigils, Jim has pursued other activities to publicize the deplorable immigration policies now being enacted by the U.S. government. He wrote a letter to officials at the Immigration Office, calling on them to be faithful to their consciences by refusing to arrest immigrants, especially if they are not guilty of criminal behavior, and he received about 150 endorsements from others. He alerted officials ahead of time of the group's plans to stand on the steps outside the I.C.E. office and read the letter out loud, though he was not sure of what their reaction might be. Jim does not plan these activities haphazardly. Aside from seeking the endorsements, in preparing for this action, he consulted an attorney as well as the press.

"We picked a Saturday because it is a slow news day, and that gives us a better chance to fill in some news. I've written a press release, but before I send it, I'm having a couple of people look at it, first." He also translated both the letter and press release into Spanish for the *Al Dia* newspaper which is published in Louisville.

Jim stood on the steps of the Federal Building on September 30, 2017, and read the letter. On October 1, *The Louisville Courier Journal* published Jim's picture, standing with several of the other 75 people who had gathered on the corner of 7th & Broadway to read and present the letter to I.C.E. officials. In it, Jim appealed directly to I.C.E. agents: "We pray for you and place ourselves in solidarity with you as you form your consciences and urge you not to follow human-made orders that conflict with God's commands." He referred to these officials as "companions in a journey toward equal justice and dignity for all . . . that welcoming strangers and loving one's neighbors is applicable to everyone, including I.C.E. agents."

Afterwards, the group walked around the corner and tried to enter the building where I.C.E. officials work, but the door was locked. He and another minister returned on Monday morning to attempt to hand the letter directly to an I.C.E. official, but no one would let them in the building. Instead, a voice from inside instructed them to slide the letter through a slot. To this day, Jim has never received a response.

In a July 27, 2017, letter to the Record, Fr. Flynn wrote: "Recently there was a video article in the New York Times. It displayed a gate in the wall between Mexico and Arizona which could be raised to allow cattle from Mexico to enter the U.S. There is no such gate anywhere on that wall to allow humans to enter." He goes on to describe a horrific incident concerning a truck that was found in Texas in which humans were discovered suffering from lack of air, intense heat and lack of water. Some of these people had died. They were fleeing the violence and poverty of Mexico. James Flynn concluded with this question: "What does this say about a society which seems to value its cattle more than its companion humans?"

The raids that I.C.E. officials began in trailer parks and other areas in Louisville where immigrants are known to live have further fueled the fire in Jim's belly.

"They come early in the morning when the guys leave for work and snatch them up. I can speak some Spanish, but I'm not bilingual, so we have some folks who are fluent in Spanish. They appear at these places when I.C.E. officials make their moves and try to speak up on behalf of those who are being arrested, as well as record what is happening. I call what I do, Solidarity in the Streets. As other concerned citizens learned of these activities, they joined in the resistance." Jim laughed. "No one has tried to run me out of town, yet. But who knows what might happen."

If anyone expects Jim to give up, they'd be wrong. His mantra remains: Resist Injustice. The members of this growing network of concerned citizens keep in touch via email, encouraging each other and expanding on their ideas.

Jim believes he can be most effective out in the streets.

"We'll see," he said with a hint of weariness. "I've done the writing to Senators and Representatives, I've sat in the offices, I've gotten arrested, but I don't want to do that anymore. I don't know if I'm doing any good or not, but we're not called to be effective, we're called to be faithful. People seem encouraged when they see us out there."

Rebecca Solnit in *Hope in the Dark* would seem to agree with Jim: "But faith endures even when there's no way to imagine winning in the foreseeable future; faith is more mystical" (64).

Ugly remarks or crass gestures aimed at Jim and those who stand witness with him do not tempt him to veer from his goals. Neither does he wish to retaliate.

"I feel sad for people who exhibit negativity toward those who are fighting injustice. I look at those people at Trump rallies, and I wonder why they can't understand how they are being used by him." Occasionally, the demonstrators receive strong support at the unlikeliest of moments. Jim recently wrote: "Yesterday, Thursday, 12/17, Fr. Joe Graffis and I held our weekly vigil on the corner of Bardstown Rd. and Goldsmith Lane (lots of traffic!!). We held our large banner: IMMIGRANTS AND REFUGEES WELCOME (with the image of the Holy Family fleeing to Egypt). While standing there we noted a car pulling into the lot behind us. A man emerged and walked over with a bottle of water and a box of chocolate covered cherries. He thanked us profusely and hugged each of us. He identified himself as from Egypt." Sometimes owners of nearby businesses bring offerings of cocoa or hot coffee on cold days.

Jim Flynn and friends marching in St. Patrick's Day Parade, Louisville, 3/10/18

Jim senses that the message of the vigils is catching on, and more people who feel angry over the deportations and inhumane treatment of immigrants will eventually join them, and perhaps come up with other ideas about how to translate their message into non-violent resistance. Jim firmly believes that, "Together we can dream of a more just world. After all, six women at Ascension Parish started by sitting around, drinking coffee, asking themselves what they could do, and look what has happened since."

Jim and his group have recently added another action intended to shine a light on this issue. For the past couple of months, four days a week, one day per each, a group stands across the street from four Catholic high schools in Louisville, Sacred Heart, Trinity, St. X, and Assumption, displaying their message.

"Our hope is that seeing the banner will prompt discussion among the students about the issue of immigration," he said.

Whenever he can, long-time friend, Rev. John Burke, stands with Jim at the corners of main thoroughfares, helping to publicize the group's message.

"Some people support us," John said, "others oppose us, but unfortunately, I also see a lot of apathy among those who drive by. It seems to me that most of them are staring down at their phones."

Jim is energized by the resurgence of political action all over the country. Many other social justice issues, such as women's rights, lack of accessible health care, the widening gap between rich and poor, and Black Lives Matter are sending people in unprecedented numbers into town halls and out into the streets, while also triggering massive amounts of emails, letters, and postcards to legislators' offices in Washington, D.C.

Jim laughed; "I've read that these postcards are causing a lot of grumbling among the legislative staffs. They're saying they've never had to work so hard to keep up with all the complaints they're receiving."

Rebecca Solnit offers a sobering warning to Jim and other activists: "Effects are not proportionate to causes—not only because huge causes sometimes seem to have little effect, but because tiny ones occasionally have huge consequences. Gandhi said, 'First they ignore you. Then they laugh at you. Then they fight you. Then you win.' But those stages unfold slowly. And as the law of unexpected activist consequences might lead you to expect, the abolition movement also sparked the first widespread women's rights movement, which took about the same amount of time to secure the right to vote for American women, has achieved far more in the subsequent eighty-four years, and is by no means done. Activism is not a journey to the corner store, it is a plunge into the unknown. The future is always dark" (*Hope in the Dark*, 61).

Rebecca Solnit is not telling Jim anything he doesn't know, because this is not the first time in his life the Fr. James Flynn has stood in solidarity with the poor and dispossessed. From his early years as a priest, he has remained faithful to the causes of social justice, even when criticized and when his actions seem to have borne little fruit. He does not give up. His activism on behalf of immigrants, his opposition to the Vietnam War, his fight for racial justice, his denouncement of the *School of the Americas*, and his stance against nuclear proliferation have occupied his mind and heart for many years. He does not expect quick or easy answers, and there's not a chance anyone will find him relaxing in his retirement chair, watching TV, proclaiming he's done enough. At 89 years of age, Jim's resolve to stand in solidarity with those who have no power remains unwavering.

CHAPTER 2

James Flynn was born in Louisville, Kentucky in 1929, the oldest of seven children. His parents were life-long Democrats who struggled financially while raising their children. He grew up in Louisville's west end in a three-bedroom home, one for Jim and his two brothers, one for his four sisters, and the last for his parents.

"My parents weren't particularly active in politics, though of course, my mother remembered a time when women couldn't vote," he recalls.

He attended Christ the King Elementary School, then left home after the eighth grade for the seminary at St. Mary's College in Marion County, Kentucky.

"That's what we did then. I think the year I left, there must have been about 20 of us, though in the end only three in that class stayed in the seminary all the way to ordination. From early on, I wanted to be a priest. I have no idea why, except that we had a couple of priests who were role models for me. My parents were happy about it. That's the way it was back then," he said.

Jim remained in contact with his family throughout his seminary years.

"I came home during the summers, and I'd get a job. I usually spent Christmases with them, too."

According to Ed Flynn, the youngest of the Flynn children, he and his siblings idolized Jim because he had left at a young age to become a priest.

"Jim was clearly the apple of my parents' eye, and for a Catholic family, his ordination was a high point in our family life. It was a big deal when he came home to visit in the summers and at Christmas. I also remember us going to visit him, with my mother packing fried chicken and ham sandwiches for a picnic." Bill and (much later) Ed followed Jim to the seminary, but both decided that the priesthood was not their calling.

It wasn't that Jim didn't struggle with whether he wanted to continue with his studies for the priesthood.

"Even though I may have wavered at times, somehow, I knew I wanted to hang in there," he said. "It was a long road, but I knew that's what I wanted. I, like everyone else, had to wrestle with the question of whether I wanted to be single for the rest of my life. In those days, the spirituality was so medieval. We were taught that the world was a terrible place, a place you didn't want to get mixed up in. The seminary was a refuge from this world, and especially from women. These weren't conscious realizations for me, not until later. Heaven and hell. Scary stuff. I bought the program," Jim said. "That's what you had to do. I accepted it. That's just the way it was. What we learned was that being single meant you could be more dedicated to the Church."

Jim also bought into the deeply-held myth that was prevalent throughout the Catholic Church: priests were special, a cut above everyone else.

"That idea was hammered into us," he said. "Over and over, on all fronts. And again, I bought it."

After ordination in 1955, as soon as he began his work in parishes, he realized that "there were a lot of nice folks out there," and he wasn't any better than anyone else. "I'd like to think I was never arrogant in my relationships with others because I was a priest, but perhaps I was."

Jim's first assignment was to St. Ann's Parish, in the Algonquin neighborhood of Louisville, where he lived with two or three other priests.

"Our rectory life, though, was not community life at all," he said. "We lived together, but it could not be considered community life."

Jim remained at St. Ann's for six years. According to Ed Flynn, the pastor "was a pre-Vatican, old-fashioned man whose attitude was, *Do what I say, or else.* From the first crack out of the box, he picked on Jim."

Jim's next assignment was as an Associate Pastor at Our Lady of Lourdes. It was here that he met several people who would become life-long friends.

In 1961, when George Kilcourse was a 13-year-old, eighth grade graduate at Our Lady of Lourdes School, he remembers, even at such a young age, being impressed by Jim.

"Fr. Flynn possessed a knack for reaching parishioners," George said. "He connected with young people by forming a youth group. He later taught Scripture study sessions for interested high school students. Jim injected energy into worship services as he began to bring aspects of Vatican Council II into parish liturgies and worship." George laughed as he recalled Jim's words one Sunday as parishioners gathered for Mass. He remembers Jim encouraging everyone, "You don't think you can sing? God gave you your voice, so give it back to God, no matter how it sounds."

Pat Geier first met Jim when she was a 10-year old parishioner at Our Lady of Lourdes Parish. When she became a high school student at Sacred Heart Academy, she joined the parish youth group that Jim was in charge of at the time. He also taught religion to her senior homeroom class.

"My entire life has been influenced by him," she said. "Other than my parents, I can't think of another person who has had more of an impact on me. I grew up in a segregated, privileged world. He introduced me to the world of the marginalized and to social activism. During my high school years during the 1960s, he took our youth group to Open Housing protests. He took us on work projects to Appalachia. He had us reading Dietrich Bonhoeffer and Harvey Cox. My adolescence coincided with the civil rights movement and anti-war protests. These were heady times. He helped me navigate these waters."

Barbara Aubrey also first met Jim when she enrolled as a sophomore at Sacred Heart Academy after her family moved to Louisville from Cincinnati. She, too, participated in religion classes taught by Jim. That was her first remembrance of this man who would later become her mentor and friend. He was her senior religion teacher, and she remembers him bringing in a Scripture scholar to offer the girls the latest in thinking and research on the interpretation of the Bible.

"Later, when I got to know him as an adult, he wryly commented, 'Can you imagine 100 teenage girls really listening to a Scripture scholar?'"

Early in the interview, Barbara drew a comparison between Jim and Don Quixote on his horse, calling them both "dreamers of the impossible dream, fighters of the unbeatable foe," never giving up. After graduating from Sacred Heart, Barbara lost touch with Jim until their paths crossed again at Our Lady of Lourdes. Barbara had become a teacher at the school where Jim was still the Associate Pastor.

"Jim would come to my classroom to share albums of Joe Wise's music and talk with the kids." She witnessed how much he cared about people.

John Burke unabashedly says, "Jim Flynn is one of the greatest people I have ever known. He is my hero." John also first met Jim when he was a member of Our Lady of Lourdes. "I had left home to enter St. Thomas Seminary when I was 14, but when I came home in the summers, Jim had begun a youth group that included Bible studies. This was new at the time. Catholics didn't study the Bible as other faiths did. He was so approachable, so funny, and so prayerful. He could even make the Latin Mass sound good."

According to John, Jim's ability to relate to others crossed the gamut of all ages in the parish, from the youngest child to the oldest senior citizen.

"All the old ladies wanted to adopt him," John remembered. "He also offered Bible studies for married couples."

When John returned home from the seminary for summer visits with his family, the rector directed the seminarians to avoid working any place where members of the opposite sex were employed.

"But Jim countered this notion," John said. "He was so balanced and took a more wholistic approach. He told us we needed to learn to relate to women, not avoid them. Women could be our friends." John paused briefly. "What a thought!" he said.

For several years, John remained a member of the youth group at Our Lady of Lourdes.

"We didn't just sit around and eat pizza, though that was fun," he said. "Jim had us perform community service. I was aware early on of Jim's commitment to social justice."

In fact, the mother of John's best friend once accompanied Jim to an open-housing demonstration which apparently had the potential to turn violent.

John laughed, "Jim made it clear to this woman that he would protect her, and if the situation became dangerous, he told her to stand behind him." John added, laughing, "The funny thing was, she was much taller than Jim."

Rev. Joseph Graffis, like John Burke, was also studying at St. Thomas Seminary.

"I felt close ties to the pastor of Our Lady of Lourdes, Fr. Anthony Gerst," Joe said, "but Jim impressed me the first time I met him. My parents got to know Jim as well. My dad was a Methodist, but he was attracted to a Bible study class taught by Jim. Both of my parents participated in these sessions." Eventually Joe's dad concluded that he "ought to become a Catholic," and Jim baptized him in a private service. Jim also presided over Mr. Graffis's funeral.

According to Joe, St. Thomas Seminary was "pre-Vatican, run like a military school." Joe joined Jim's youth group when he returned home during the summers and sensed that things could be different.

"He was young, engaging and excited about Vatican II with its emerging emphasis on the liturgy and Scripture. We were excited because Jim generated a lot of discussion about the Church. We were a close-knit group, and Jim kept track of the progress of Vatican II documents. As his enthusiasm transferred to us, he became a role model for all of the young people in the group."

Joe stayed in touch with Jim throughout his seminary years, during which time he and some of his fellow seminarians participated in the anti-war and the civil rights movements in Baltimore.

"His legacy will be his passion for justice and solidarity with the poor. He never wanted to become a typical pastor, but instead he identified with the poor and disadvantaged."

As John Burke's image of the priesthood evolved, Jim became his ideal of what a priest ought to become.

"He nailed it for me," John recalls. "I remember thinking, if this man embodies what it means to be a priest, sign me up. He's prayerful, he cares for all people, and he is concerned about social justice."

In 1972, John and another former member of Our Lady of Lourdes parish were ordained. Before they celebrated their first mass, they met with Jim to seek his advice at this important juncture in their lives.

CHAPTER 3

In 1962, Pope John XXIII convened the Second Vatican Council to look at ways of bringing the Catholic Church into the 20th century. As this pope expressed it, he wanted "to throw open the windows to the rest of the world and allow in some fresh air." When Jim left Our Lady of Lourdes after six years to become an Associate Pastor at Mother of Good Counsel Parish, he and Rev. Dick Fowler were appointed as co-directors of the Worship Office, which placed them on the cutting edge of implementing Vatican II.

"He received a lot of flak from people who resisted change, not only his parishioners, but other priests as well," John Burke said.

During this time, seeds were sown in Jim's and Dick's hearts and minds that would eventually lead to the establishment of a new parish, literally from the ground up.

"The two of us went through the old regime together in the seminary," Jim said, "and when Vatican II burst onto the scene we became very interested in what this Council was saying to the Church and the world."

After marrying Tom Aubrey, Barbara had stayed home to care for their children, and during Jim's tenure at Our Mother of Good Counsel parish, he'd stop by occasionally to visit.

"He often gave me commonsense advice," she said. "I mentioned to him once that I had always wanted to be a missionary, and he said, 'Barbara, look around you. This is your mission.' He helped me see the importance of my mission as a mother."

By the mid-60s, along with his intense interest in Vatican II, Jim had also come to believe that the Vietnam War was immoral, mostly through the influential writings of Thomas Merton and Martin Luther King, Jr.

"These men influenced me greatly," he said. "While I was at Our Lady of Lourdes, my activities irked a lot of the parishioners. Not only was I speaking out, I was also marching and demonstrating in the streets with others against the war and on behalf of open housing."

Many parishioners leveled heavy criticism toward Jim because of these activities, and he felt disappointed when he'd get wind of it, though he had expected some of these reactions.

"They didn't confront me directly," he said. "They complained to the pastor. But Fr. Gerst was supportive of the things I was doing."

Vatican II was opening windows and calling on the church to move forward in response to the cries of the world, and Jim was listening. He believed it imperative to be in the world and take seriously the griefs, sorrows and anxieties of his parishioners, and to offer them substantive, compassionate, and realistic responses to their suffering.

Because of these desires, Jim became eager to learn more about the emergent Biblical revolution happening in the Church, so instead of taking vacations in the summers, for three or four years, he attended classes at the Biblical Institute in Chicago, where a thought-changing idea gradually began to take shape in his mind: *The Bible is not to be taken literally*. One professor taught him something that left a lasting impression.

"Sacraments are signs and symbols and not substitutes for social justice," he said. "Those words resonated in me with a beautifully sibilant sound, and that's one reason I remember them. I learned the context for many passages in the Bible, and this helped me understand they were not to be taken literally. My teachers contextualized events that had occurred in the Old Testament."

These dawning realizations led Jim to explore and understand the deeper meanings contained in Scripture, which in turn influenced him to speak out on social justice issues.

"Faith had to have feet, it had to take flesh, and not just remain in the head or heart. This was all so refreshing and exciting to me, because I grew up with the literal interpretations of the Bible."

Jim also studied under Fathers Barnabas Ahern and Carroll Stuhmueller, both Passionist priests and teachers at Bellarmine College in Louisville, Kentucky.

"I studied Israel's prophets, and this led to even more radical shifts in my thinking."

Of any decade in recent memory, the 60s are probably the most exciting and memorable years for many people, as they were for Jim.

"The 60s were the beginning of it all for me," Jim said. "The most formative. Because of the Second Vatican Council, the Vietnam War, Open Housing and the Biblical Revolution I had become immersed in, I experienced profound changes in my thinking."

In the book, *No One's Easy Daughter*, a School Sister of St. Francis captures some of the excitement: "We heard Bob Dylan's iconic *The Times, They Are A-Changin'*—for us they certainly were—and Joni Mitchell's *Both Sides Now*. We would be challenged to look at both sides, not only of life and love, but of almost every *given* in our lives. Civil rights struggles, with their Black Panthers and the Chicago Seven; the Vietnam War in which many of our students fought and some died; the Cuban Missile Crisis; the assassinations of JFK, MLK, and RFK; the construction of the Berlin Wall, Communism in Russia and China; Mao's disastrous Cultural Revolution; the Space Race; the beginning of the Information Age; systems thinking and chaos theory; Vatican II, of course, and an influx of transformational theological thinking and books; the death of God movement. In Africa alone, 32 countries gained independence from their European rulers during that single decade." (*No One's Easy Daughter*, 114)

Fr. Jim Hargadon shared Jim Flynn's and Dick Fowler's enthusiasm, and the three of them embarked on a journey together to open themselves to new ways of thinking and apply what they were learning to their daily lives and activities. They spent hours discussing the issues.

Jim said, "The excitement generated by Vatican II, as well as many other exploding cultural changes, compelled us to figure how to integrate these new teachings and ideas into our roles as priests."

Encyclicals are official documents written by Popes to explain, teach, and expand upon the Catholic Church's positions on a variety of topics. Jim closely studied these papal communications to broaden his knowledge and understanding of their important messages, and their influence on his thinking remains today.

According to Jim, a wider and deeper understanding of Scripture had begun to emerge in 1943 with the encyclical, *Divine Aflante Spiritu,* though the full significance of its words did not drift down through the Church until the late 50s. The movement away from strict literalism was introduced with this encyclical, whose English title means, "With the Help of the Divine Spirit." Issued by Pope Pius XII on September 30, 1943, it called for new translations of the Bible based on the original languages in which they were written instead of the Latin Vulgate of Jerome. Pius XII noted that advances had been made by scholars studying archaeology and engaged in historical research, which made it advisable to further define the study of the Bible.

This encyclical created a rift between those who wanted to cling to the Bible's literal interpretations, and those who, after studying Hebrew and Oriental languages, had begun to understand things differently. Because Hebrew and Oriental languages were closer to the original languages in which the Scriptures were written, some scholars moved away from literal interpretations. Pope Pius XII finally stepped in and said the Church needed to accept the interpretations of Scripture scholars rather than theologians. Upon issuance of this encyclical, more priests began to study original languages which, in turn, brought about changes in their understanding of the Scriptures. But it took years for this information to filter down to local clergies.

Jim said, "I had only been ordained for four years when these new thoughts began to emerge. I was pretty green, and it was exciting to me."

Another major encyclical, issued by Pope Paul in 1968, sparked heated debate among Catholics. Pope John XXIII had appointed a commission to study the controversial issue of the use of artificial contraceptives, but he died before the group finished its work. His successor, Pope Paul VI, received the recommendations of the Pontifical Commission on Birth Control, a commission he had expanded when he became Pope. At the end of their work, despite the commission's recommendation that he broaden the Church's position on the use of birth control, on July 5, 1968, Pope Paul VI reaffirmed the orthodox teaching of the Catholic Church regarding married love, responsible parenthood, and the rejection of most forms of artificial birth control. Looking back at this encyclical on its 50th anniversary, in the June 2018 edition of *Commonweal*, Paul Baumann stated, "Pope Paul VI followed a minority-report, warning that for the church to admit it had erred in the past would fatally undermine its authority and credibility" (10). The encyclical, *Humanae Vitae*, shut the door on any further discussion of birth control.

"That's when a lot of priests and nuns began to leave the Church," Jim said. "We knew that many people were wrestling with whether to have more children. They knew they didn't want more children, couldn't afford more children. We were hearing the grass roots struggles with this issue. But Rome wasn't paying any attention. Some priests instructed people to follow their consciences, but this placed them at odds with some Church officials. They were ordered to instruct their parishioners to follow *Humanae Vitae.*" According to Paul Baumann in *Commonweal*, "Unable to embrace the church's teaching on birth control, many priests, religious, and Catholic parents retreated from answering questions about the church's teachings on sexual morality, both inside and outside the family."

Unable to reconcile their consciences with the official teaching of the church, some of Jim's classmates left the priesthood, though he was not tempted to do so.

"I felt empathy for them," he said. "I understood why they were leaving. I admired their courage. But I wanted to stay and fight. I wore the collar with a certain sense of pride, though it was mixed. I knew that a lot of people did not appreciate the Church, but a lot of people did. I realized then that no institution is perfect. I felt that if I hung in, I could do good. There was a saying going around at the time, my country right or wrong, and many people felt that way about the Church, my Church right or wrong. But we know that neither of those is true. The Vietnam War exposed the United States as a very human institution and Vatican II did the same for the Church. They were both human institutions, subject to many mistakes."

Many years later, in the October 19, 2018, issue of *Commonweal*, p.11, Paul Baumann expanded on Jim's thoughts when he raised the question on the minds of many Catholics of whether they ought to leave the Church in light of the sex abuse scandal that has ripped through the institution.

"How can we justify staying?" he asked. "I think the answer is similar to the one you might give when asked to justify allegiance to the United States of America, a nation founded as a slave state and established by the virtual annihilation of its native population, a country that killed several million Vietnamese in an unprovoked and unjust war and now threatens the peace of the entire world by putting nuclear weapons in the hands of a clearly repulsive and disturbed individual. You remain because, despite the nation's manifold sins, you still want to believe in the truth of the propositions put forth in the Declaration of Independence, the Constitution, and the Gettysburg Address. You stay in the church, despite its sins, because you long for what it proposes about the nature and destiny of human life to be true as well."

CHAPTER 4

Epiphany Parish was created to carry out the ideas being promulgated by Vatican II, such as the emerging role of the laity, the emphasis on social justice, and the call for liturgical reforms.

"What Dick Fowler and I wanted to do was start from the ground up, literally, with a community in a building that reflected these new ideas," Jim explained. "Parish membership would not be limited to people living in the area surrounding the church. Anyone was welcome, and its members would not be forced by geography to join or be restricted from joining. We wanted the foundations of this new church to be a focus on social justice and a liturgy that engaged people. The U. S. Bishops had released a statement that said, 'Good liturgy fosters and nourishes faith, while poor liturgy weakens and destroys it.' That was a motif for us, engaging people in singing and a full and active participation in every liturgy."

During the late 60s, they began to develop their plans for bringing this new parish into fruition, but it wasn't until 1971 they approached Archbishop Thomas McDonough to see if, and how, they might move forward.

Many older priests were adamantly opposed to Vatican II with its sweeping calls for change, but even though Jim and Dick were young, Archbishop McDonough trusted them. He knew they had taken a leading role in helping other priests understand the new theology and liturgies. The Archbishop was also listening to Vatican II's calls for conversion, and he knew that it was incumbent upon the Catholic Church to move forward. As a result, despite strong opposition, the Archbishop readily accepted their willingness to take this risk. Jim and Dick were particularly keen on the idea of forming a parish that wouldn't need to reform itself, but from its beginning would execute the directives of Vatican II.

Joe Graffis said, "Jim was always the radical, pushing the envelope for change. He hoped to establish these four pillars at this new parish: a renewed and deeper understanding of Scripture, more participation by the laity in the liturgies, more leadership by the grassroots members of the Church, and an increased emphasis on social justice."

Jim Flynn added, "We wanted to stress the importance of religious education of all adults, youth, and children as a foundational element of the parish."

John Burke remembers the talk surrounding this new venture.

"They had no intention of having a school connected to this parish," he said. "A school tends to suck up a lot of the resources of a parish. Instead, Jim and Dick wanted to accentuate life-long formation. They hired a Youth Minister; they were concerned about social justice; they emphasized liturgical excellence, with music being a high priority; they fostered an ecumenical awareness, with connections to their neighbors as well as their brothers and sisters in other churches. This parish wouldn't be an island; instead it was to be leaven in the community."

During the search for an appropriate location, on one cold day in January, the two priests, at the Archbishop's suggestion, scoped out a piece of land in the Bashford Manor area.

"When we looked at it, we both knew this was not the place we were looking for," Jim said. "But Dick said to me, 'Hey, this happens to be the Feast of the Epiphany, and there's not a parish by that name in the diocese. Why don't we call it Epiphany?' And that's how it got its name."

Eventually their quest led them to the beautiful place where Epiphany Church would evolve, a piece of property located in eastern Jefferson County already owned by the Archdiocese where the old St. Thomas Orphanage still sat. Long before the first brick would find its spot, Dick and

Jim began conducting Sunday Mass in the gym of the orphanage. But some logistical problems arose from the very beginning. For example, an annual picnic took place every August to raise money for the orphanage, and at this time the parishioners had to vacate the premises during which time Jim and Dick concelebrated an outdoor Mass for the approximately 200 congregants who had already affiliated themselves as parishioners. The following weekend, when they returned to the hot and stuffy gym for Mass, the memory of celebrating Mass outside had planted seeds that would not be forgotten. The next year, when the picnic again temporarily displaced the congregation, Jim and Dick concelebrated Mass under an open pavilion located on the property.

Larry Melillo, an architect and a congregant at the time, had been consulted earlier about his ideas for this new church and he asked, "Why couldn't we just pick up this pavilion and surround it with glass for our new church?"

Eventually Mr. Melillo answered his own question, translating into physical reality the Church of the Epiphany as it is today.

Becoming members of a parish close to their home, Barbara and Tom Aubrey had lost touch with Jim.

"I was not experiencing spiritual enrichment or community involvement as a member of this parish," she said. One evening, she was introduced to the pastor of Middletown Christian Church. During their ensuing conversation, she explained her disappointment with her parish, and he mentioned that his church might be a place of interest, describing the variety of programs it offered. "I found myself startled, and I remember thinking, how could I ever leave my Catholic Church?"

The next morning, Barbara's telephone rang, and when she picked it up, Jim Flynn was on the line. She had not spoken to him in at least a year. He asked her if she was okay because he had recently dreamed that she was calling out for help. As she relayed her conversation with the Middletown Christian pastor, she realized she did indeed need Jim's help. He told her that he was starting a class at Our Mother of Good Counsel on Vatican II and the new Dutch Catechism and suggested she attend the sessions.

"I took his advice, hired a babysitter, and went to the classes," Barbara said. "At the end of the course, Jim celebrated Mass with the participants standing around the altar. It was wonderful."

That evening, he told her that he and his friend, Dick Fowler, were being given the opportunity to begin the first Vatican II parish in Louisville.

As the parish developed, Jim regularly shared with Barbara the dreams for Epiphany.

"Every week he'd call and update me as their ideas progressed," she said. "It was so exciting. They had chosen to establish the parish on Archdiocesan property in Anchorage and use the nearby orphanage for a temporary home and gathering place."

The first night they moved in, Jim called to invite Barbara, her husband, Tom, and their daughters to come over and see their new home.

The parish grew quickly numbers-wise as the physical structure began to take shape. The walls were constructed in a circular pattern surrounded by large panes of glass, and rather than pews, worshippers sat in moveable chairs, which contributed to making the space more flexible.

"Instead of looking out through stained-glass windows, we reveled in scenes that reflected the changes of the seasons," Jim said. "The idea was to prevent us from closing ourselves off, to keep our gaze focused on the outside world of which we were a part. We also knew what a beautiful piece of property we had, and we wanted to take full advantage of its beauty. We were in tune with nature and creation. Perhaps that decision was more prescient than we could have imagined, given that Pope Francis's encyclical, *Laudato Si*, was recently written to remind us of the importance of creation and the environment, and our need to preserve it and stay connected to the earth."

When George Kilcourse was a seminarian, he spent his 1974 summer internship at the Church of the Epiphany, shadowing Jim for three months while the parish worship center was being built. (George admired how often Jim reminded everyone that the community was the "Church" and the Worship Center was the "house for the church" where the assembly gathered for liturgy and other events.)

"Long before the ecology movement, Jim was observant and protective of the natural environment," George reported. He remembers one incident that summer after a terrible storm. He and Jim were out on the grounds near the construction for the parish's Worship Center, observing the loss of several large trees.

"When the new church building was built, it had no steeple," Barbara Aubrey pointed out. "People couldn't imagine why. But Jim explained that God is not an 'up there' God but lives with us and in us. Also, there were no kneelers. Jim explained that Vatican II called for us to stand during the consecration because the members of the community were full active participants. It was an empowering and fresh way of celebrating the Eucharist."

Barbara and her husband decided to become an integral part of Epiphany.

"Jim asked me to fix coffee the first Sunday to encourage parishioners to stay after Mass and get to know one another. One thing I noticed about Jim was that once he meets you, he never forgets your name. He knows you forever. As a priest, he refused to put himself above anyone else. In fact, he'd often tell us, 'Get us off those pedestals.'" Barbara remembers Jim's homilies. "He told us we must not just listen to the message of Jesus, but we must live it every day."

Pat Geier had gone on to study at Eastern Kentucky University, but she returned to Louisville after graduation and joined Epiphany Parish.

"It was an exciting time to be Catholic," she remembers. "With the liturgical changes of Vatican II, Jim and Dick Fowler brought the liturgy alive. They emphasized that liturgy must be an expression of our work for justice and peace. Jim's homilies never failed to hammer home the point that Jesus made a preferential option for the poor, and that's our work as well."

David Horvath met Jim in 1981 at Epiphany when he and his wife went to the service held one week before Easter Sunday.

"I had heard such good things about what was happening in this parish," David said, "and my wife and I wanted to check it out." Upon their arrival, they introduced themselves to Jim, and the next time they returned, Jim greeted them by name. "I was surprised that after I'd only met him once, he remembered our names. It blew me away," David said. "I didn't know at the time that Jim's tenure as pastor was coming to an end, and our new baby was baptized in May by his successor. But we stayed connected with Jim from then on."

Sr. Carmelita Dunn, SCN, knew Fr. Flynn mostly by reputation when she served as the principal of St. Frances of Rome Elementary School in Louisville.

"I had asked Jim to come and speak with my teachers and students," she said. "I wanted them to hear from him good quality theology."

When Epiphany opened, Dick Fowler and Jim Flynn hired her to offer community outreach for the parish, part of which contained the Berrytown and Griffytown neighborhoods, both of which were comprised largely of African-Americans.

"I wanted to model what I did after the Sister Visitor Program which at that time was active in the west end of Louisville," Sr. Carmelita said. "I applied for a grant to carry out the mission of helping provide people with necessities, and Tom Breslin supplied me with a little Matador to drive to places I needed to go. Dick Fowler rode around with me to familiarize me with the area I'd be serving. When the parish officially opened, Dick and Jim visited every family in these communities and left a Bible with each household. Many of the people remembered them both long after they had left."

Part of Sr. Carmelita's job was to welcome people.

"At times, ministers of other churches in the region thought I was evangelizing, trying to turn people into Catholics," she said. "But I wasn't." Gradually, good relationships formed among all the churches in the area. "We gained a lot of respect from other religious traditions," she said. "Epiphany parish often held ecumenical worship services. Jim and Dick also participated in pulpit exchanges with ministers of non-Catholic churches. Jim's interest in her parish activities impressed Sr. Carmelita. He would take the time to ask her about her ministry.

Sr. Carmelita was impressed that Jim led a wholesome and well-balanced life.

"He enjoyed the outdoors, hiking, running and biking. He seemed to enjoy life no matter what he was doing," she said.

George Kilcourse agreed.

"Jim was a role model for others in that he would often get up and ride his bike for miles, long before others were even awake," he said.

According to Sr. Carmelita, Jim's commitment to people living on the fringes of society remained extraordinary.

"Jim was the first pastor to hire a social responsibility minister, one whose job was to work to foster social justice among its member," she said. What is now known as the Eastern Area Community Ministries was begun at Epiphany. "There were a lot of poor people in plain view of the church," Sr. Carmelita said, "and we wanted to reach out. One important aspect of Jim's capabilities as a leader was to always ensure that his staff had the knowledge they needed to implement new programs. I remember how he created opportunities to meet with our Protestant neighbors to discuss their thrust into social justice issues. He sent staff to workshops to obtain the most up-to-date information, so they could understand new ideas and processes."

Sr. Carmelita provided an example.

"One time, we traveled to the Kirkridge Ecumenical Center in Pennsylvania to broaden our understanding of how to strengthen relationships with other churches in the area," she recalled. "Kirkridge advertised itself as 'a place to be and to become a people of hope, compassion, justice and service.'" According to Sr. Carmelita, "Everything is important to Jim, including people, keeping up with the times and, getting correct information."

In the early 70s, in what many believed to be a misguided attempt to integrate the public schools, Louisville began busing students from one end of the city to another.

"These were scary days," Sr. Carmelita said. "There was a lot of anger on the part of white people because of these changes, and sometimes threats were made. Jim would attend gatherings to pray with people who were frightened, to stand with them. I was concerned about him at times. But Jim was a risk-taker, a person who took the Gospel seriously."

Joe Graffis expands on this idea.

"Sometimes Jim gets close to the edge," he said. "He's a prophet who says things that others might not say. He's outspoken. He doesn't want to be where he can't do that. He wants to be where he can speak out. Jim has lived justice and solidarity with the poor."

George Kilcourse agreed.

"Moving on from Epiphany, his ministry at the African-American parish of Holy Cross Church in west Louisville took him back to his old family neighborhood. But many changes had occurred in this area that once boasted one of the largest Catholic populations. Catholic parishes and schools had been closed and the needs were many. During the 1960s when racism erupted in west Louisville, Jim had stood among African-Americans, joining their protests." On one occasion, George remembers, "Jim called a friend who was a Disciples of Christ minister. He even loaned his Roman collar so that people would recognize the Protestant minister as a peacemaker, like Jim."

"I considered him a marvelous leader," Sr. Carmelita concluded. "He knew how to help people participate in understanding new issues. He knew how to put faith into action. But he does everything in a quiet manner. He doesn't draw attention to himself. He exerts strong leadership in a quiet manner. He is a wonderful person, there is no getting around that!"

While serving at Epiphany, Jim became aware of and began to study *Liberation Theology*.

"I had heard from people who were returning from trips to Latin America that many were being killed in those countries, and I didn't know why. The search for answers led me in the direction of *Liberation Theology*." Gustave Gutierrez's writings resonated with Jim, and he began to realize that the huge gaps between the rich and poor in these small countries were being caused by the military, political, and economic policies of the United States. "Our efforts in social justice were aimed not only locally, but also to the larger world. I saw it as my task to raise awareness of the local and global inequities."

George Kilcourse completed a doctorate at Fordham University in 1974, then studied pastoral care for a year at Mundelein Seminary and the University of Chicago Divinity School before ordination. When he returned to Louisville and reconnected with Jim, he was impressed by his mentor's ability to pioneer *Liberation Theology* in the parish. Jim facilitated a group of parish men to read and discuss Gustavo Gutierrez's *Liberation Theology*. He awakened these men, corporate executives and business professionals, to Catholic social justice teachings in the context of Third World nations.

"He had so many skills," George said. "He emphasized the importance of life-long learning, especially keeping up with the new methods and insights of Scripture scholarship. Jim is no doubt, the best self-educated priest of his generation in the diocese." George further emphasized, "In preaching and teaching, Jim tapped into images from the Scripture that had long lain dormant. As a liturgist participating in national conferences and one with national contacts within Peace and Justice circles, he had the kind of mind that integrated his learning. He has fine interpersonal skills and actively engages people. Jim's ability to remember a face and even names, demonstrates the sensitivity of his pastoral care."

Because of the parish's progressive political stances, some people refused to attend Epiphany; others left when they realized what this church stood for.

Jim said, "We hired a full-time director of religious education for both children and adults. We were trying to implement the teachings of Vatican II with its emphasis on social justice, and this was so new to people that it hit some of them hard. But many others believed in and understood the Church's mission in this area."

Parishioners were also attracted to the type of music in the new liturgical services, sometimes using guitars and other non-traditional instruments. Others were turned off by them.

"I remember on one of our first Sunday worship services, one gentleman came to the door, took one look at the guitars sitting on stands close to the altar, and turned around and left," Jim laughed. "He was a well-bred man, but this was not his kind of church."

Rev. Michael Casagram walked through the door of the Retreat House at Gethsemani at 3:00 PM, the exact time the scheduled interview was to begin. After finding a room in which to talk that would not cause a disturbance to any of the retreatants, he pulled out his notes, and with no prodding, started to share his recollections of Jim.

"From the time when I first came to know Jim until this day," he said, "he has always been a person who sought to live the gospel. Fr. Flynn is one who not only proclaims but lives the Gospel. He is where the rubber hits the road is my best way of describing him."

Fr. Casagram addressed what he called the great danger of power and wealth in the Church and society.

"Jim has worked tirelessly to unmask aspects of these realities because of how they blind humanity to what living our faith is really asking of us. Jesus has told us clearly enough, 'Not everyone who says to me, Lord, Lord will enter the kingdom of heaven, but only the one who does the will of my Father in heaven' (Mt. 7:21)."

Michael began his life as a monk at Holy Cross Monastery in Virginia in 1961, but later transferred to Gethsemani in 1964. Shortly after coming to Gethsemani he attended conferences being given by Thomas Merton to the novices and junior monks at that time. Early on he was asked to assist in printing, collating and typing up articles that Merton was preparing to publish. Merton was an important formative influence in Michael's life then and ever since. He was then sent to Rome to study theology during 1974-1977.

"I met Jim when I returned from Rome. I experienced some hesitation on the part of my community to have me ordained. I had the theology I needed but fell short in my ability to communicate it effectively. After conferring with Fr. Eugene Zoeller, a professor at Bellarmine University in Louisville, he suggested that I participate in an RCIA Program (Rite of Christian Initiation of Adults) at Epiphany Parish where Jim was the pastor. Jim helped me to apply what I had learned in Rome to the everyday life of the Christian today. I'd spend every Monday through Wednesday at Epiphany, then return to Gethsemani for the rest of the week. This went on for about seven or eight months until the new members in the program were baptized or fully received back into the Church."

From the beginning of his time at Epiphany, Michael appreciated the way Jim got up early each morning to jog.

"He led a monk's life," he laughed. "On the days I stayed at Epiphany, I accompanied him in rising early, and after a cup of coffee, going out on a four to seven-mile run. I respected his discipline. We also prayed and enjoyed meals together, either the two of us or with friends. During these times we shared many valuable conversations."

During the RCIA classes, Michael admired Jim's ability to facilitate discussion among the members of the group.

"He had a way of freeing them to ask whatever questions they were struggling with in seeking baptism or reestablishing their Catholic faith. He did not want them to accept superficial understandings of what they were seeking.

He wanted them to speak their minds about anything that may have bothered them about the Scriptures or becoming a Catholic. He wanted them to be authentic, not just go through the motions."

After the RCIA sessions ended and Michael was no longer spending time at Epiphany, he and Jim stayed in touch.

"When I was asked to leave Gethsemani to assist with one of our new monasteries in Venezuela, Jim was quick to encourage me to take advantage of the opportunity. I became interested in the political scene of what was happening between the United States and other Latin American countries like Bolivia, El Salvador and Venezuela where I was headed. The involvement of the United States in these countries was often detrimental to their own search for freedom and the best interests of their people. It was the whole corrupting influence of wealth and power all over again. The dire poverty I encountered in Venezuela was like the conditions Jim experienced in Central America. We shared common interests. I think Jim may have met Ernesto Cardenal in Nicaragua. Cardenal had been a monk at Gethsemani earlier in life but because of poor health was advised to leave in 1959 by Thomas Merton. He also advised him to return to Nicaragua because of the great need for improving the social conditions in his native country."

Sometimes when Michael comes to Louisville, he and Jim spend time together.

"In fact, I recently met with him on one of my trips with another monk from the Abbey, our 95-year old Brother Frederick. We ended up bearing witness with Jim on Shelbyville Road across from Trinity High School, where he and others were holding up signs to welcome the stranger and to raise awareness of the hurtful immigration policies we have in this country. Jim has also spoken to the community at Gethsemani about the lasting effects of Oscar Romero's life and death in El Salvador."

Fr. Casagram believes that Fr. Flynn has worked hard at giving pastoral witness to the great insights and clarification of Church doctrine taught by the Second Vatican Council.

"Pope Francis has emphasized many of these same issues. An instance of this is the way he has reached out to those who are divorced and remarried, telling them that the decision about whether to receive the Eucharist is a matter of following their own consciences," Michael said. "Fr. Flynn has helped many who are dealing with painful situations in their lives. People insist on dogma, and the Church must stand for certain things, but Jim shows us how to apply authentic teaching to the real issues facing society, where our faith applies to our everyday lives. The preferences of the wealthy and privileged too easily blind our eyes to the basic needs of so many who are poor and lack the necessities of life. Jim helps us to see where our authentic freedom lies, both in the Church and in the larger society, and his concern for social justice remains steadfast."

In keeping with the Archdiocese of Louisville's policy to reassign pastors after they had served in a parish for 10 years, Jim left Epiphany.

"It was hard to leave," he said. "I felt like it was my child. So many of the parishioners had accepted the theology we were trying to convey through our preaching and our ecumenical outreach. We had solid relationships with some of the Protestant churches in the area. I appreciated the support I had received from so many. But I knew it was time to leave. The parish needed some new blood."

The Archbishop appointed Fr. Joe Graffis as the next pastor at Epiphany, and he continued to strongly emphasize and support the social justice ministries that had begun during Jim's tenure. David Horvath was attracted to this work and he and his family had joined the parish.

He said, "Epiphany had made a deliberate choice to have a full-time social justice minister on its staff. Eventually I became involved in that ministry and became the Chair of the Social Responsibility Committee."

CHAPTER 5

In 1981, upon his departure from Epiphany, Jim was granted a sabbatical, and he used the time to travel to Israel as part of a study group that lasted from July through November of 1981.

"This trip was a good experience for me," Jim said. "It enhanced my understanding of Scripture. I had been studying on my own, but this trip deepened my understanding because I touched the places I had been reading about. For example, when we went to the Sea of Galilee, I could see where Jesus stood and looked down the hill at the crowd when he delivered the Sermon on the Mount as told to us in St. Matthew's Gospel. And when I was in Jerusalem, walking the way of the cross, these experiences gave me a feel for who Jesus had been."

Rev. John Burke added, "During Jim's six-month sabbatical in Israel, he delved deeply into Scripture. As a result, he came to believe that a concern for the poor should be central to our Christianity. He became more radicalized."

Jim believes that Jesus was a political figure.

"When he called out the Pharisees as being 'hypocrites,' he was making a political statement. They were in bed with the Romans, and Jesus knew exactly what he was doing," he said. Jim used the term quisling, defined as a person who collaborates with the invaders of his own country. He said, "Quislings cooperated with the Nazis during World War II, and some Pharisees were quislings. People who do not believe the Gospels are political haven't read them carefully."

When Jim left for Israel, he knew little about the situations in Central America. He did not know that Bishop Oscar Romero had been assassinated in El Salvador. He had heard that four women had been murdered, but it wasn't something that he paid a lot of attention to at the time. In 1982, during a retreat at Gethsemani, Jim spent time in the cemetery next to Thomas Merton's grave. The monks also allowed him to make use of Merton's hermitage. During this retreat, it became clear to him that he needed to make some radical changes in his life, though he had no idea what form they would take. Another event occurred around this same time that affected him deeply. His good friend, Fr. Dick Fowler, died. This sequence of events all happened rapidly: his Sabbatical in Israel, his retreat at Gethsemani, and his friend's death.

"My life was shaken, and I knew that I could not return to a normal parish. Coincidentally, I heard that the priest at St. William's was leaving. As I struggled to discern a path for my future, I received a call from the Personnel Director of the diocese to fill in as the 'Sacramental Moderator,' the new term for pastor, at St. William's, in June of 1982."

Little did Jim realize how his decision to accept this position would change his life. As he stepped through the doors of St. William's Parish, he couldn't have known that he was being called to an ever-deeper understanding of social justice and what that would mean in terms of fully committing himself to the poor, the disenfranchised, and those who have no power. He was about to become immersed in Central America, a part of the world he knew little about. And he would take on a more public face.

CHAPTER 6

In 1982, shortly after Jim moved to St. William's Parish, a priest friend of his from Pennsylvania, Fr. Bernie Servil, who had been working in El Salvador, asked Jim if he could address the parishioners about disturbing events that were taking place in Central America. Three young people who had been forced to flee El Salvador accompanied Fr. Servil to share their stories. As the group described the military oppression and violence which they, and thousands of others in their country, as well as Nicaragua and Guatemala were enduring, Jim listened and was profoundly touched by what he heard. During this meeting, the visitors introduced the congregation to what was being called the Sanctuary Movement and invited St. William's Parish to join its ranks. Just beginning to take root in the United States, Presbyterian religious communities in Tucson, Arizona, spearheaded this effort to provide homes for those fleeing persecution in Central America. Since it was just getting off the ground, there were few Sanctuary communities in the U. S. at this time, but after hearing these horrific stories of war and upheaval, St. William's parishioners considered the possibility of becoming one of them.

After thoroughly considering the legal and moral issues involved, St. William's voted to become a Sanctuary parish. Wanting to be above board throughout the process, parish leaders informed Archbishop Thomas Kelly of their intention, and he said to them, "Do what you have to do. You know you are running a risk but do what you have to do."

Map of Central America

Because harboring immigrants was considered an act of civil disobedience, they also told the immigration officials in Louisville of their decision.

Taking the next step, the congregation applied to the Sanctuary community in Tucson, and shortly afterwards, one of the Arizona groups notified the St. William's community that a family of three needed a safe shelter, and they were ready and willing to come to Louisville.

"At the time, we referred to this movement as another *Underground Railroad*, modeled after what African-Americans had set up during the Civil War to help slaves escape," Jim said. In the company of members of the Tucson Sanctuary Movement, the family left that city and traveled east for a couple hundred miles to their next destination, then continued moving secretly from city to city until they reached Nashville. When they arrived there, Jim and a group from St. William's drove down, picked them up, and transported them to Louisville.

The fact that this event occurred on December 10, 1982, which happened to coincide with the second Sunday of Advent that year, provided an ironic twist to this story.

"We were struck by the timeliness of their arrival," Jim recalled, "because of course, one of the hymns we sang as part of the Advent liturgy was, *O Come, O Come Emmanuel.* The young man's name was Manuel and his pregnant wife's name was Maria. Along with their two-year old daughter, Mara, Manuel and Maria came into our midst at the perfect time in the liturgical cycle." The three of them moved into the rectory in December, and their baby was born in February. Because several women involved in the movement at St. William's happened to be named Patricia, Manuel and Maria named their daughter, Patricia.

One of those Patricias happened to be Pat Geier.

"When Jim left Epiphany, I followed," she said. "St. William's was engaged in so many social justice activities. They still are. What stands out for me was our work in the 1980s in solidarity with the poor in Central America. My hands-on involvement with refugees—above all my first experience in Nicaragua and later Guatemala—those were formative, unforgettable experiences. Once you have those kinds of experiences, you're never the same. You 'can't go home again.' The many months he spent in Nicaragua and Guatemala changed Jim. He fell in love with the people there and his love for them has never wanted."

Manuel, Maria, Mara, and Patricia lived at St. William's for several years. Parishioners took turns providing clothing, food, and medicine, and meeting whatever other needs the family had. For the first few months, members of the parish spent nights with them, because if immigration officials showed up with deportation papers, a plan had been set in place to expose their actions. When the St. William's parishioners had decided to join the Sanctuary movement, wanting to be transparent, they had also notified the local press and their local congressperson, Rep. Ron Mazzoli, who was cooperative in many ways, though other politicians at the time were not. This decision was part of the overall strategy to raise awareness of the situation in El Salvador and help explain why people were being forced to flee.

Manuel, Maria, Mara and Patricia were not the only immigrants to take advantage of St. William's hospitality during the time the Sanctuary Movement was active.

Jim said, "We welcomed and housed many others, some who stayed for several months, others who may have stayed only four or five days."

The motives behind the political strife in Central America during these years were confusing to Americans. The Reagan Administration presented U.S. citizens with its version of the events taking place in these countries, a version which happened to be at odds with the stories being told by those who traveled to and spent time there. After a brutal, 30-year war, an insurgency under the name Sandinistas had overthrown Nicaragua's dictator, Somoza. The Somoza family had taken charge in Nicaragua in the early thirties and remained in power until 1979. Franklin D. Roosevelt had said of this brutal dictator, "He's an SOB, but he's our SOB."

The Reagan administration lost no time in labeling the Sandinistas a dangerous communist movement. The civil wars raging in Guatemala and El Salvador, according to the propaganda coming out of Washington, were also driven by communist ideology. Reagan purported that if the revolutions in Central America were successful, the southern borders of the United States would be at risk of being taken over by communism.

Because there was so much confusion, Jim decided he wanted to travel to Central American to ferret out the facts for himself. Religious people had been advised not to travel to El Salvador and Guatemala because it was considered too dangerous. Bishop Oscar Romero had been assassinated and four Maryknoll nuns had been killed. Though the U.S. government opposed the new Nicaraguan regime, the Sandinistas themselves urged anyone affiliated with a religious institution to come and visit their country. The fact was that Catholicism was woven into the fabric of this new government. Four Nicaraguan priests were high-level members of the Cabinet.

Jim was part of the first delegation to visit Nicaragua in June of 1984 with about 100 people in a group calling itself, *Witness for Peace*. Hoping that officials from the U. S. might also be interested in learning the truth of what was occurring, WFP invited at least one person from each Congressional district to accompany them, believing this would be the best way to counter some of the propaganda, but only a few Senators or Representatives ever availed themselves of this opportunity to view the situation first hand.

Upon his arrival in Nicaragua, Jim was touched by the poverty, but also the beauty and simplicity of the people he encountered in his travels. He moved around the country, meeting with people and witnessing for himself events that he had only heard others speak about. Shortly into his stay, he learned that a group of young men who had been killed in the war were being brought down the mountain to Managua to be buried. Jim and other *Witness for Peace* delegates were invited to the funeral. Here is how he described what occurred:

> "On July 3, 1984, the Witness for Peace office in Managua received a call from a military base inviting a few WFP delegates to the funeral of those Nicaraguan soldiers the following day . . . we were honored to be asked, and gladly went to the funeral. We sat in a large auditorium with caskets arranged in front, weeping family members sitting in chairs nearby. We sat immediately behind them. The military ceremony was conducted, and when it was over we delegates were privileged to hear Carlos Mejia Godoy sing, 'Ay Nicarague, Nicaraguita.' It was the first time I had heard this beautiful song composed by Godoy, though I have heard and have sung it many times since."

After the song, Jim said that everyone in the auditorium was crying. Across the aisle from Jim, a young female soldier was in tears, "tears of pain and pride."

After the service, Jim and the others were "surprised and honored" to receive an invitation to meet with Tomas Borge, the commander of Nicaragua's military forces.

Jim continued, "Then he uttered words that I'll never forget. While I can't quote verbatim, he said, 'Today (July 4) in your country you are celebrating your independence from Britain. Congratulations on 200 years of that independence. Now I wonder why your leaders do not want us to have our independence from 40 years of the Somoza dictatorship. Your government is supporting the contras and you see the results of such support in this funeral of young patriots from Managua. Like your ancestors, we are struggling to free ourselves from so many years of brutal repression. All we want is to be free and to find our own way to that freedom. I urge you to continue the work of Witness for Peace and continue to make efforts to change U.S. policy toward Nicaragua and be partner in our struggle for independence.' Tomas Borge got up, shook each delegate's hand warmly, and left us, marveling, wondering and deeply touched." Every July 4, Jim recalls Tomas Borge's words, "Both as memorable and as a challenge to WFP and others to struggle to change U.S. policies in Latin America and allow those countries to develop their own kind of independence as Tomas Borge urged us so heartily."

In November of 1984, Jim and Pat Geier organized the first *Witness for Peace* delegation from Kentucky to visit Nicaragua. While there, members of this organization from other states who were in Nicaragua learned that Reagan was proclaiming to the American people that pictures of MIGs sitting on a ship off the coast of Corinto had been taken, and because they knew not to trust President Reagan's version of events, WFP delegates pitched tents on the beach to observe the situation first-hand. At the time, Jim, Pat and others from Kentucky were traveling in a different part of Nicaragua, but when they learned what was happening, they decided to join the WFP delegates in Corinto who had camped out on the beach. What they observed was that these MIGS looked suspiciously like large farm equipment.

"We took pictures of the objects and called home to tell others what we saw," Jim said. "What we were looking at was a shipment of large combines and tractors, and it was then we realized that Reagan was stirring up trouble by telling the American public they were enemy planes."

While in Corinto, the WFP delegates also received word that a U.S. frigate was sitting out in the water off the coast, and they decided to get in a boat and sail out for a closer view.

"We rented a small, rickety boat," Jim said, "and reporters accompanied us. I remember one was from the New York Times, and a couple of others represented TV stations." After about a half-an-hour of traveling, an imposing black silhouette of a ship came into view, which, according to Jim, "looked like Darth Vader."

Jim laughed as he recalled this story.

"One of the delegates was from North Carolina, and he picked up a megaphone, and in his pronounced Southern drawl, shouted, 'Y'all go home.' Though they probably couldn't hear us, the boat hightailed it out of there in a hurry. That was an important act of non-violence. It was dangerous for us, but WFP had informed the crew ahead of time who we were, and they wanted no part of any confrontation with 30 U.S. citizens in the Caribbean. It could have turned into a political disaster for Reagan if anything had happened."

By the time he returned from his second trip, Jim realized that the Reagan Administration was making a concerted effort to keep Nicaragua poor by tagging it a communist country as a justification for refusing to support the Sandinista Government. Because Jim was concerned and wanted to continue exploring the issues, he applied to become a long-term delegate with *Witness for Peace*. These were unusual activities for a parish priest, and Jim felt grateful for his parishioners' patience each time he felt the call to return to Central America. Members of the St. William's congregation remained as puzzled as other Americans about the events happening in Central America, because reports coming back from those who were witnessing the strife first-hand did not match the inflammatory rhetoric being presented by the U.S. media, or what President Reagan was telling the American people.

Upon returning from Nicaragua, Pat Geier was motivated to speak out.

"After that, I did a lot of public speaking around the southeast trying to convince other churches to declare as Sanctuary members," she said. "St. William's was very public about it." Pat also flew to El Paso, Texas, to pick up two children to bring them to a relative from El Salvador who was already living in the United States. "I was a little anxious about it," she said, "but the border was not as militarized and tight as it is now."

Though he clearly felt the call to serve with *Witness for Peace* on extended trips, Jim once shared these words with his congregation: "I enter this part of my life's journey with some feelings of hesitation. I don't particularly want to leave St. William's, I don't want to leave home, my routine of running to start each day, working, skiing, meeting, and all the thousand-and-one other little 'ings.' I enjoy being in my own familiar surroundings. I have found it difficult to learn Spanish at 56 years of age, obviously harder than it would have been at 36. But somehow, despite all the hesitations, I know in my heart of hearts that I must go. It is a call I can no longer ignore or postpone."

Over time, though David Horvath had remained a parishioner at Epiphany, he also became more engaged with Jim and his work with the Sanctuary Movement at St. William's.

"Many at Epiphany were passionately involved in social justice work, but in a less radical manner than at St. William's," he said. "I was fed and nurtured by Jim through contact with him at St. William's."

David, a long-time librarian at the University of Louisville, chose not to travel to Latin America with some of the early delegations including *Witness for Peace*.

"I felt I could not bear the poverty and the devastation that I knew I'd encounter," he said. "It would have broken my heart."

Instead, he immersed himself in the grass roots organizing and administrative aspects of the movement, such as coordinating emails, phone trees, and organizing the myriad of details that were required for others to be engaged and involved.

"I admired the frontline people," he said. "I'd always send them off with my blessings, though I felt I couldn't be one of them."

Meanwhile, Epiphany continued to deepen its own involvement with Latin America. Social Responsibility Minister Jack Jezreel moved forward with a project called, *twinning*.

"We intended to pair up with an African-American parish, an Appalachian parish, and a parish in El Salvador," David explained. The wars in Central America raged on, and people involved in the movement in the U.S. were still hearing horror stories about the atrocities happening there. David continued, "We became paired through the Washington-based SHARE Foundation with Our Lady of Lourdes Parish in Calle Real, El Salvador in January of 1990. The war lasted for two more years. I was changed forever from those experiences."

Jim volunteered to go to Nicaragua for seven months with *Witness for Peace* from July of 1986 until February of 1987. Archbishop Thomas Kelly supported Jim's activities.

"He was an empathetic guy, and he understood that people were called in different directions. My activities were considered completely off the wall for a diocesan priest, but on the other hand, very consistent with my understanding of working for social justice for the poor and ostracized of this world. These desires had been percolating in me for some time."

In fact, when some skeptics learned of Jim's activities, they began to refer to him as a "kook." Archbishop Kelly was not among them. He clearly stated his support for Jim's work. In an interview published in an April 5, 1990, article in *The Louisville Courier Journal*, Archbishop Kelly said he "was glad to have a chance to talk about Flynn. I don't have to examine every point he's on. It's possible that we might have different views on some of them. That doesn't matter. What it comes down to is that Fr. Flynn is someone who naturally cares about the people of Central America. He is a priest who really cares, and he has just done a great job. We don't think he is a kook at all. We appreciate him."

During the seven months he was there, Jim stayed in touch with his parishioners via letters. As much as he could he wanted to let them know what was going on. In the same April 5 *Louisville Courier Journal* interview, Jim said, "People (at St. William's) have had a patient endurance with my type of leadership—or whatever it is. They have given me room to do these kinds of things."

Members of *Witness for Peace* sometimes traveled to areas in Nicaragua where actual fighting was occurring. Every few weeks, after these experiences, they would return to Managua to debrief and check in with each other.

Jim laughed quietly.

"Here I was in my fifties, and I felt I was just starting to get the hang of what being a Christian was all about. These times out in the countryside were intense. People couldn't stay too long because of what we saw and heard. It was scary and distressing. And the physical limitations were difficult, such as not having access to medication. As you might suspect, we were plagued by bacteria that caused diarrhea and giardia, which left us weak."

Jim witnessed some difficult situations. One time he was out with a fellow delegate with *Witness for Peace*, traveling in the mountains from one town to another. Piled into the back of a truck with "maybe 30 other people," they drove up a hillside to a village of 10 or 20 houses, and the people told them that the contras, militants who were supported by the

U.S., had tried to burn down their school. Several people were injured, but no one was killed. In the next couple of days, in a second village, they saw evidence of another attack by the contras. A little girl, around four or five years old, had a bandaged arm, and they learned that her parents had been killed by the contras.

"I can still see the shock on that little face," Jim said.

In November of 1986, Jim was visiting a family in the mountains of Nicaragua when they heard a story on the radio. He remembers it this way.

"The host family and I were listening to the radio when we heard a story about a U. S. plane that had been shot down, killing two of the pilots. Nicaraguan soldiers had captured a third. A picture had been taken of the U.S. soldier being led from the crash site by a Nicaraguan soldier.

But not all stories were grim. Jim remembers an incident told to him by a fellow priest, concerning an elderly woman who was quietly watching the construction of a school being built in her small village. Providing a good education to its citizens was a primary goal of the Sandinista Government, and Nicaraguans were hungry for education, including older, uneducated people. Someone leaned down to this elderly woman and asked her if she knew how to read and write.

"Not yet," she responded, with a smile.

The Sandinistas developed policies to improve the lives of all citizens of Nicaragua. They sent people out from the cities to the small villages to teach people to read and write, but the contras, in their attempts to stop the Revolution, killed these teachers. In Nicaragua, in 1983, a husband and wife were out in their fields picking coffee when a group of contra soldiers killed them, another attempt to erode any advancements of the Sandinista Revolution. The Ministry of Health developed programs to improve the diets of Nicaraguans. They also instituted agrarian reform by dividing large plantations into areas that were given to poor people. The U.S. opposed these policies.

"These practices are still happening," Jim said. "Agrarian reform continues. People now have small plots of land on which to grow their own crops. The U.S. continues to interfere through the war on drugs. The drug dealers negatively influence these governments, especially today in Honduras."

The chief financial interests in Latin America were bananas, coffee, and sugar. Chiquita was the largest grower of bananas. Rich men from the U.S., like Dick Cheney, sat on their Board of Directors, all of whom were donating to politicians in the United States. Large companies were owned and operated by rich families, and the poor were used to perform the labor needed to harvest the crops.

Jim lamented, "We just want to buy our cheap bananas, and get our coffee cheap, and we think it's our prerogative to operate in the way that best suits what we see as our national interests."

Reagan's administration continued to promote the idea that whatever appeared to be against U.S. interests was communist. His assertion that the dangerous spread of communism would reach the borders of the United States was what drove his policies.

"But it was really all about money," Jim said, holding his hand out and rubbing his thumb and fingers together in the universal sign for greed. "Reagan referred to people who were killing Nicaraguans as 'freedom fighters.' This made it difficult to distinguish who the real freedom fighters were. This was true in Nicaragua, El Salvador, and Guatemala. Revolution was happening in all three of these countries, though in El Salvador and Guatemala the uprisings were being crushed by their respective governments."

Jim observed first-hand the damage wrought by the United States: the destruction of barns, water facilities, and burned-out buildings. The people were scared by U.S. planes flying overhead and expected to be bombed.

"Many couldn't understand why the United States was arming the contras," he said. "On one trip, near the Honduran border about 20 WFP delegates stood hand-to-hand with Nicaraguans to affirm our solidarity with them, and we made it clear that we did not condone the support the U.S. was offering to the contras."

Jim's struggles after his seven-month stay in Nicaragua with *Witness for Peace* prompted him to return to the U. S. and begin to organize delegations to Nicaragua. During his seven months in Nicaragua, each time he had returned to Managua, he and the other delegates had continued to discuss their sadness and anger toward the U.S. government, which energized them to get word back to those in the United States who would listen to the truth of the situation, contradicting the propaganda that was being reported by many U.S. news outlets.

"We were appealing to anyone who would listen to talk to their congressmen and women about what was truly happening," he said, "and some did."

Back home, Jim tried to share what he had seen and heard, though he was often met with a great deal of skepticism by people who thought he had been indoctrinated by the Sandinistas.

"But I had been told by others to tell people what I had seen and heard with my own eyes and ears. If they chose not to believe me, so be it," he said. "My own family didn't believe me, even though I had seen these things with my own eyes. They had listened to Reagan's propaganda. 'Do you not believe your government?' some asked."

Ed Flynn echoed his brother's sentiments.

"You know, we just didn't believe the government was lying," Ed remembers. "And the more flak Jim caught from the mainstream, the more confused we became. We suspected Jim was a victim of his own innocence and naivete." According to Ed, their family had the normal amounts of sibling rivalry, though it could become particularly contentious between Jim and Bill, the middle of the three brothers, with Jim taking the liberal side on issues, and Bill, the conservative. "The rest of us didn't believe him either. We'd ask him, 'What are you doing, come on now, you can't really change things.' But no matter how heated the arguments became, they usually ended amicably, with everyone still speaking to each other."

Ed admits, "At times we may have even been embarrassed by him. We believed he was wrong, and it was incredibly frustrating." Ed says that some of Jim's siblings were closer to Jim's point of view than others, but "all of us thought he was misguided to one degree or another."

Members of Jim's family weren't the only ones upset by his actions. Some thought he was a Marxist who was being duped by the Sandinista Government. Many people believed he was too critical of the United States. According to the April 5 *Louisville Courier Journal* interview, when six priests were murdered in El Salvador on November 29, 1989, Jim received a picture of them from an anonymous source, accompanied by this note: "Here's what happens to your left-wing buddys. Your next." Though the poor grammar and misspellings prompted Jim to laugh, he said, "It's never pleasant to receive anonymous, threatening notes."

Jim also came under surveillance.

In the same article, the reporter, Dick Kaukas continued: "Back in 1985, when St. William's was serving as a sanctuary for people who had fled from Central America and entered the United States illegally, Flynn's personal offices were broken into and his files examined." Nothing was taken, but it looked to Jim like whoever had conducted the search had arranged papers on his desk to take pictures of them. Some suspected it was the work of the FBI. A few years later, it was revealed that FBI agents had conducted surveillance on several groups in Louisville who had opposed U.S. policies in Central America, and St. William's was one of them.

As the trips to Central America expanded to include El Salvador and Guatemala, some of Jim's parishioners began to grow weary.

"I came home in February of 1987, and I was so moved by the whole experience that I kept repeating the same stories over and over. My preoccupation with the devastation I had witnessed was foremost in my preaching. I'd show slides that I had taken to anyone who would listen. The people of St. William's knew what I had been through, and most of them were sympathetic, though not all. I understand that I probably went on a bit too much."

In Lent of 1988, in imitation of an event that had occurred in Nicaragua, Jim and some of his parishioners organized what was known as a Via Cruces, a Way of the Cross. A Maryknoll priest, Miguel Discoto, Minister of the Exterior in Nicaragua, the equivalent of the Secretary of State in the U.S., had organized a Via Cruces from the south of Nicaragua to the north, and Jim wanted to repeat this experience in the U.S. Joined by others, he organized a walk from the Tennessee border to Louisville. For various reasons, some dropped out, while others stepped in.

"There were about five of us who walked the entire route," he said. "Several churches offered shelter in their basements when we were in their towns, and they fed us."

Jim organized two of these long marches, one in 1988, another in 1989.

During one of Jim's trips to Nicaragua in 1989, after about a week, the WFP delegation went to Guatemala for another week.

"Such a beautiful country," he said. "I loved Guatemala. Nicaragua could be so hot, but we spent time in the mountains of Guatemala, where it was much cooler." Jim organized another delegation of about eight members to travel to Guatemala in 1991. "We visited San Miguel Acatan, the site where Sr. Diana Ortiz had been captured and tortured because we wanted to show solidarity with the people there. When we came into the town we were expecting trouble because the people were frightened of us. No one wanted to talk about what had happened. We had taken a vial of dirt from Sr. Diana's motherhouse in Owensboro, KY, and poured it on the earth in San Miguel."

Sr. Diana Ortiz, a member of the Ursuline order, served as a missionary to San Miguel Acatan and in 1989 was abducted by members of the Guatemalan army, detained, raped and tortured for 24 hours before being released. Jim was later arrested at the White House during a demonstration in support of Sr. Diana. When officials told the protestors to disperse, they wouldn't, and they were arrested.

"But we only spent a few hours in jail," he recounted. "I was arrested once in Washington and again in Louisville. It seems strange to me, now. During my many trips to Central America during war and violence, I never spent any time in jail." The arrest in Louisville occurred in Senator Mitch McConnell's office during a demonstration against Congress for allocating money to support the contras. "But again, we spent only a few hours in jail."

In November of 1991, Jim went to Guatemala with *Witness for Peace* for another three months. "I am still friends with the two guys I worked with during this time." His task was to arrange trips for people who wanted to travel to Guatemala to experience what was going on. It was dangerous work, and because the Guatemalan Government was spying on them, they had to be careful when they reported back to the WFP office in Washington.

Jim said, "Hundreds of people took advantage of these opportunities to visit Guatemala, all in small delegations. These were not easy trips. I remember one particular journey when a woman was so upset by what she saw she was on a flight back to the states in two days."

By this time, Jim had reached his early sixties, and it was time once again for him to be reassigned.

Rev. John Burke said, "Jim initiated important changes during his time as pastor at St. William's. For one, he brought the altar to the middle of the church. No presidential chair for him! Jim also created the atmosphere for openness and acceptance of all people. At St. William's today we welcome all worshipers, gays, lesbians, and transsexuals."

It should also be noted that though the Catholic Church still barred women from ordination into the priesthood, they took on vital roles in the ministries at St. William's, and continue to do so to this day.

Chapter 7

Jim was granted some time off for another sabbatical, and because he hadn't been assigned to a specific parish, he received an invitation from some close friends.

"It was my husband who invited him to move into our office/apartment over the garage," Barbara Aubrey said, "and he stayed for about six months. He became a very important part of our family. We were honored that he was the celebrant at our daughters' weddings and funerals for our parents."

When his brief sabbatical ended, his next assignment was to Ascension Parish where he stayed for about a year before asking to be assigned to St. Martin de Porres. While there, he continued his trips to Central America.

"I went to El Salvador for the first time in 1993 with a delegation of about four or five people from Epiphany." By this time, the Sanctuary movement had wound down. The wars in Central America were ending, and because peace accords had been signed in El Salvador, the civil war was over. However, fighting persisted in Guatemala.

Over the next 10 or 12 years, David Horvath continued in his local organizing efforts, while also remaining involved with the parish in El Salvador. In order to coordinate and collaborate their efforts, several organizers, Jim Flynn and David among them, formed an umbrella organization that became known as the Louisville Area Council on Central America, or (LACOCA).

"Jim is not a natural collaborator," David said. "His gifts are two-fold. He has an idea and throws it out there to see where it will land. Then he waits to see who is with him or not before moving forward. His is always the prophetic voice. He leads from the front, but always gives credit and appreciation to those who follow. Administrative details and logistics are not his strong suit. He remains true to himself and the issues that call him, and he calls others to hear the same message."

As an example, David points out Jim's recent decision to stand in vigil in front of the I.C.E. office in downtown Louisville to protest I.C.E. enforcement policies based on fear and prejudice.

"When he decided to do this, it didn't matter if others chose not to accompany him," David said. "He went by himself. Eventually others came too."

In the 1990s, Pat Geier devoted a good deal of her attention to the turmoil in the Middle East.

"I was involved early on in the movement against sanctions and later the war in Iraq. In the late 70s, Jim served on the Steering Committee of the Fellowship of Reconciliation, and he encouraged me to join. We had the privilege of working for many years with Jean and George Edwards, the co-founders of FOR in Louisville. I first learned about the Israeli/Palestinian conflict from other FOR members and became immersed in that issue. I straddled my work with the Middle East and my concern for Central America."

Through the years, as part of her professional work as a licensed clinical social worker, Pat has worked with hundreds of undocumented immigrants to secure immigration waivers to prevent families from becoming separated and loved ones deported to their home countries to face the violence of poverty and war.

According to David Horvath, though the efforts to expand the vision of the social justice movement in Louisville have grown to include the broader issues affecting black and brown people around the world, Jim's focus has remained on Central America and immigration.

"He has stayed involved with Spanish-speaking communities, raising lots of awareness and engagement to help them. He is a wonderful preacher and storyteller. These are by far his best organizing tools. He attracts people to the cause by being an effective writer, and he tells a great story. He stands at the pulpit and lets the chips fall where they may. His messages are often subversive and dangerous, if you listen carefully to what he is saying."

Jim organized and led delegations to Central America in the late 80s, throughout the 90s, and early into the 2000s. Needing a change, he took an opportunity to assist in a parish in Park City, Utah.

"I spoke enough Spanish to help out with the Hispanic population in the area. Between 2000 and 2009, I organized three delegations to Central America, and I participated in two trips with Maryknoll priests on retreats to visit the places where priests and nuns had been killed in El Salvador and Guatemala. That was a sobering experience. In fact, one of the priests who was killed in Guatemala during the war, Fr. Stanley Rother, has now been beatified."

George Kilcourse observed, "Jim is ever creative and responsive to immigrants and refugees. He visits them often, he baptizes their children, and presides at their funerals. He is a uniquely gifted shepherd to them."

LACOCA eventually broadened into KITCA, the Kentucky Interfaith Taskforce on Central America.

"Jim was very involved with *Witness for Peace* and *Pastors for Peace*, founded by Rev. Lucius Walker," David said. "He worked tirelessly with these groups to sponsor caravans to Central America and Cuba to highlight the failure of U.S. policy and the embargoes the United States had imposed on Cuba. It was known as 'People's Foreign Policy.' During the 90s, Jim also traveled to Guatemala to accompany refugees who were returning to the areas in their country from which they had been driven out by the military during the war." David paused for a second to emphasize his next words. "This was dangerous work," he insisted. "Jim risked his life to do this."

George Kilcourse couldn't agree more, saying, "Jim made many trips to Central and South America as a peacekeeper in solidarity with those enduring unjust sufferings. His courage was unflagging as he accompanied refugees back to their homelands. All the while, Jim's eyes were wide-open as he learned and brought back to us insights and evidence of his ongoing conversion to serve the needs of people who were called 'the disappeared' where the military had slaughtered them and hidden their bodies in remote areas. After Jim returned from one such long-term mission on a Saturday evening, he looked forward to the Sunday morning Eucharist. In his homily, he briefed us on his actions and the conditions in places like El Salvador, Guatemala, and Nicaragua. He emphasized his service to others, not himself as a person. As I listened, I realized Jim was telling us the message of Jesus: 'Christ must increase, I must decrease.' (John 3:3). He often mentions the Jesuit martyrs, their housekeeper, and her daughter from the University of Central America. These martyrs, unjustly robbed of all human dignity, have awakened us to the cost of discipleship."

In 2008, in the Chixoy Dam area of Guatemala, the government forcibly removed people for no other reason than they considered them to be in the way. During the Rio Negro Massacres, as many as 5,000 indigenous people were killed. Jim traveled to Guatemala to stand in solidarity with these people, and David's son, Jason, accompanied him on one of these delegations.

"Jason still says even today that his life has been forever marked by these experiences with Jim," David said.

KITCA further expanded to include people of the Caribbean region, and became known as KITLAC, the Kentucky Interfaith Taskforce on Latin America and the Caribbean, which Jim had formed into a 501C3.

"When Jim moved out to Utah, he turned the organization over to its remaining members," David said, "and we actively pursued the goals of the group for many years. I lost frequent touch with Jim while he lived in Utah, but when he returned to Louisville, he and I picked right up where we had left off. He was engaged in fewer projects, but he and I became stronger colleagues, friends, and allies in all the right struggles. I sometimes play his technical advisor, helping him with things like computer issues and opinions about his latest ideas. Most recently, he has become engaged with the environment through *Laudato Si*, Pope Francis's encyclical on the environment, the struggle for immigrant justice, and leading edge, a broad spiritual cosmology."

In 2011, Jim and three couples, David and his wife being one of them, planned a trip to Nicaragua.

"We gathered for dinner a few times to discuss our itinerary, and when the trip was over, Jim asked if we might continue to meet as an intentional community. We now try to share dinner twice a month to discuss everything from 'praying the news,' to current events, to death and dying, to cosmology, and all points in between. All topics that happen to be of great interest to Jim."

Jim ceased his travels to Central America in 2014.

"Mostly for medical reasons," he explains. "These experiences were totally transforming for me. Having been there and fallen in love with the people, I've just never been the same. It's a gift to go to places like Central America, and I can only reiterate that I fell in love with the people. I'd love to go back, but age prevents it. My doctor cautioned that if I broke a leg, or sustained another type of injury, it would be difficult to receive adequate medical care."

Barbara Aubrey eventually became involved in a weekly Archdiocesan Catholic television network, and part of her job was to conduct interviews with a variety of people on issues that were of interest to Catholics.

"On our program, Studio 19, I'd often invite Jim to share his activities in Central America," she said. "One of my co-workers couldn't understand why I was doing this. At first, he expressed reservations because he viewed Jim as being against the government. But as he listened to Jim over time, he came to me and said he now understood the importance of Jim's message."

CHAPTER 8

Maria Scharfenberger lived in Peru for two years with the Ursuline sisters during the late 1980s, during which time she felt an intense call to understand the Latin culture. It was a life-changing experience for her. She became acquainted with *Liberation Theology*, and while there, she participated in parish life led by lay people who had formed women's groups, youth groups, and human rights groups.

"The people participated in making decisions about their lives, trusting that what they decided was what God wanted for them," she said. "Living with the sisters taught me about walking in solidarity with the poor."

When Maria returned to the United States, she felt as if the bottom had dropped out of her life.

"I experienced shock and grief," she remembers. "I had become accustomed to quiet time, to being immersed in reflection on Gospel living. It was during this time that I started attending services and participating fully at St. William's Catholic Church. This is where I met Jim Flynn."

She and Jim began to converse and share their experiences, leading to the formation of a small community group that met about twice a month. They discussed the difficulties involved in "fitting in" to American society after having experienced the dire poverty and harsh conditions they had encountered in Central and South America. In *No One's Easy Daughter*, a School Sister of St. Francis attempts to explain this phenomenon:

"Every summer I did something to learn more Spanish and understand the different cultures of Latin America. One summer I spent eight weeks in Honduras, where I practiced the language, but I learned much more than Spanish. I remember that I spent most of my time crying over a poverty I had never seen. Honduras is where I discovered that if I stripped myself naked and gave away all that I had, I could not be poor in the way these people were poor because of my life experiences and my education. I was grateful for what I had and humbled by what I needed to do to share from the abundance of what had been given to me. I left profoundly changed, and the desire to live a simpler lifestyle has stayed with me over the years." (pp. 155-156)

This same sister eventually went to work in Peru, and she writes of her time there: "It was easy to live a simple life in Paita, where everyone was pretty much in the same situation, and I didn't have to face materialism as I do here in the U.S. To live counter culturally here is a daily decision and never easy." (pp. 157)

Maria Scharfenberger faced this same dilemma when she returned from her time in South America.

"I became close to Jim," she said. "He understood where I was coming from."

During their times together, Jim told Maria stories of his experiences with *Witness for Peace*.

"I was aware at the time of the difficulties in Central America, but I was unaware of the role that the U.S.-backed contras were playing in the wars happening, there," Maria said. "Jim began to educate me."

As a result, Maria decided to travel to Guatemala with a *Witness for Peace* delegation.

"I had been with Jim and others from the United States when we visited the refugee camps in Mexico that were set up when Guatemalans fled the fighting in their country. But I had not been to Guatemala."

Maria ended up staying for two years.

"I learned so much about Jim during this time," she said. "He is a gentle pusher, and his passion for peace and justice is contagious. I got pulled into his excitement and his hopefulness for making change. He challenges you to step up. He is so good with people, such a good listener, and he remains upbeat despite whatever difficulties he faces."

Maria was present when the *Witness for Peace* delegation visited San Miguel Acatan, the site where Diana Ortiz lived when some members of the Guatemalan military captured, raped, and tortured her while she was making a retreat at a center near Guatemala City. She affirms Jim's recollection of how scared the people were, and of their reluctance to speak about what had happened.

"We tried to be careful," Maria said. "It was a spooky experience. We did not want to put the people there in any danger by talking about issues that could have gotten them in trouble with the authorities."

Jim remembers, "There was a saying among those of us who were working in Guatemala at the time, 'Walls have ears.'"

CHAPTER 9

Jim's father infused his life with meaning by often telling his children as they sat around the dining room table, "We've got to take care of the little guy."

"Of course, even then, I knew he was referring to more than size," Jim said. "But because I am small in stature, I used to wonder if his remarks were also aimed at me. My parents were poor. They went through the Depression, two floods, evacuation of the west end, and their struggles to take care of their seven children affected me. Politically, my father was a Democrat; he knew that Democrats were on the side of the poor. He admired Roosevelt and saw him as a savior in many ways because he passed Social Security. I just knew that my mother and father had a tough time. But they made ends meet. My siblings and I often talk about that. And here we are."

Ed Flynn tells it like this, "I believe he received his psychological inheritance, his spirit of empathy, from Dad." He reiterated the quote from Jim, "Dad always reminded us to take care of the *little guy*." Ed remembers some of the political issues his dad talked about, particularly how the British took advantage of the Irish and how much he admired Franklin D. Roosevelt and Al Smith. "I'd describe Dad as a dyed-in-the-wool, New Deal Democrat," he said.

Fr. James Thompson, one of Jim's professors in the seminary, also exerted a strong influence on Jim and was instrumental in teaching the importance of encyclicals that shaped his thought.

Jim said, "The social encyclicals he taught affected me a lot. They were centered on working people, which caused me to reflect on my father and how he struggled to raise a family without ever receiving an adequate wage. In 1891, the Church had addressed these issues in an encyclical, *Rerum Novarum* and again in 1931, 40 years later in *Quadragesimo Anno*, on that same theme, adequate wages for workers."

Pope Leo XIII issued *Rerum Novarum* (translated from the Latin to mean of the new things) on May 5, 1891. This encyclical enunciated the late 19th-century Roman Catholic position on social justice. Its three major themes were the balance between labor and capital, the common good and the role of the state.

John Augustine Ryan, a priest born in 1869, worked tirelessly during his priesthood on behalf of social justice, especially for the right of workers to be paid a just wage. In his article in *Commonweal's* July 6, 2018 issue, author of "Social Justice Warrior: The Legacy of John A. Ryan," Arthur S. Meyers writes:

> The challenge for the church was to champion the cause of the poor without endangering the common good. It had to oppose socialism but not ignore the call for social reform. In Italy, the bishop of Perugia, Cardinal Gioaccino Pecci (later Pope Leo XIII), hoped to find a remedy for socio-economic problems, and found inspiration in the natural law philosophy of Thomas Aquinas. He would become the first pope to seek a comprehensive program of economic and social reform, convinced that the Holy See had to speak out on problems of the day. (17)

Later, in the same article, Meyers writes: "Rerum Novarum was a document on which a whole social program could be based."

Quadragesimo *Anno*, (Latin for in the 40th Year) issued by Pope Pius XI on May 15, 1931, sought to clarify and expand on the principles outlined in *Rerum Novarum* which it credits for the spread of regulation securing the rights of workers and the emergence of Catholic labor unions among many other benefits. This encyclical discusses the ethical implications of the social and economic order. Pope Pius XI describes the major dangers for human freedom and dignity arising from unrestrained capitalism and totalitarian socialism/communism. He also calls for the reconstruction of the social order based on the principles of solidarity and subsidiarity, a principle of social organization that holds that social and political issues should be dealt with at the most immediate (or local) level that is consistent with their resolution.

In 1991, Pope John Paul II issued *Centesimus Annus*, Latin for the hundredth year, on the anniversary of *Rerum Novarum*. It is part of a larger body of writings known as Catholic social teaching that trace their origin to *Rerum Novarum*, and ultimately to the Scriptures. The reoccurring themes of social and economic justice mentioned in *Centesimus Annus* articulate foundational beliefs in the social teaching of the Catholic Church. Throughout the encyclical, the Pope calls on the state to be the agent of justice for the poor and to protect human rights of all its citizens, repeating a theme from Pope Leo's *Rerum Novarum*.

It is easy to understand why these encyclicals have shaped much of Jim's thinking on social justice. Arthur S. Meyers also wrote of Fr. Ryan, "John Augustine Ryan was a priest both ahead of his time and for today," words that could just as easily be applied to Jim Flynn.

"I remember learning about Fr. Ryan," Jim noted.

Arthur Meyer adds some final thoughts about Fr. Ryan, which also describe Jim Flynn:

> John Ryan drew from deep roots of social justice, the words of a remarkable pope, and opportunities provided by far-sighted bishops. Recognizing the importance of broadening his own education, developing social reform efforts in practical, humane ways, and following a deep commitment to democratic values, he brought together the institutional structure and evolving teachings of the church. He created an enduring framework, which included the important principle that "equally competent workers should be rewarded equally. (20)

Teilhard de Chardin's writings attracted Jim.

"We weren't supposed to be reading him," Jim said. "When my parents sent gifts, they'd enclose books by de Chardin in the boxes. We were also influenced by Dorothy Day of *The Catholic Worker* movement. Additionally, we learned about the *Priest Worker* movement in France where priests were going into the factories to work alongside the workers to experience the conditions for themselves. It wasn't just one thing, but a lot of little things that built up in me over time," he said.

Jim remains an avid reader, though he adds a caveat.

"I don't read novels," he said, but, "Thomas Berry is someone whose books I read, as well as Brian Swimme, a cosmologist. I love his writing because I am very interested in the new cosmology story. I like Richard Rohr's writings as well. He's done a great job of popularizing the new cosmology."

John Burke sums it up succinctly, "He never stops reading."

George Kilcourse knows that a first visit to Thomas Merton's grave at the Abbey of Gethsemani, "had a powerful effect on Jim. The March 18, 1958 event of Merton's encounter with strangers in downtown Louisville also guides Jim and many others."

> In Louisville, at the corner of Fourth and Walnut, in the center of the shopping district, I was suddenly overwhelmed with the realization that I love all these people, that they were mine and I theirs, that we could not be alien to one another even though we were strangers. It is a glorious destiny to be a member of the human race . . . there is no way of telling people that they are all walking around shining like the sun . . . If only they could all see themselves as they really are, if only we could see each other that way all of the time. Then there would be no more war, no more hatred, no more cruelty, no more greed.

When asked if there are any parts of his life he might live differently, Jim says, "I'm glad I chose the direction I did, and it's taken twists and turns that I never even dreamt could happen. When I started out as a young priest I thought I'd be repeating the pattern of the traditional role of the parish priest. But it hasn't turned out that way. And I'm glad it didn't."

Jim's curiosity leads to constant learning. He meets with close friends, Rev. George Kilcourse, Rev. Joe Graffis, and Rev. Joseph Mitchell, a Passionist priest who teaches meditation and other subjects at the *Earth and Spirit Center* located on the grounds of the Passionist Monastery in Louisville, across the road from Bellarmine University.

"My friend and mentor," says George, "knows how to penetrate the world's many illusions and touch reality. In that sense he lives as a contemplative. Few have recognized so many of the illusions that blind and imprison us."

George tells this story.

> "We received a call from the Sisters of Loretto. They knew of a young El Salvadorian farm laborer in rural Kentucky diagnosed with a fatal brain cancer. Could Jim accompany him on the flight home to El Salvador, so he could be reunited with his family? Jim did not hesitate. His Spanish-speaking skills meant he was able to respond and converse with this young man. On the plane, Jim sat next to him, comforted him, held him and assisted him with walking when they had to change planes. Tenderly, gently, Jim cared for this man, providing him with the dignity that he deserved."

Service to the priesthood can be lonely, at times, but Jim has created a sense of community among some of his fellow priests.

"He has encouraged us to be ourselves," George said. "He has thrown out a lifeline and tells us to keep on keeping on, that we owe it to ourselves and others."

During Lent of 2017, Jim made another retreat at Gethsemani and attended sessions during which speakers shared teachings on Pope Francis's environmental encyclical, *Laudato Si.*

"I really enjoyed those sessions," he said.

Despite Jim's decision to curtail his travels to Central America, immigration remains his passion, and even at the age of 89, he continues to meet and strategize with people who share his concerns over the current administration's anti-immigration policies.

Jim Flynn, 2017

Chapter 10

Jim maintains his long commitment to the Latino community in Louisville and is beloved by many of them. He was happy to learn of the development of the La Casita Center, located at the site of the now-closed St. Philip Neri Church at 223 E. Magnolia Avenue. Karina Barillas, its Executive Director, describes it as a Community of Latino Hospitality whose mission is "to enhance the well-being of Louisville's Latino community through education, empowerment, advocacy, and wellness. The work is not associated with any one parish."

Though his humility cautions him to downplay his role in the founding of La Casita, Karina claims otherwise, saying, "Fr. Flynn was instrumental in helping us figure out what to do. He offered advice and guidance on how to bring it into being. But he never offers his opinions unless I ask for them. He is so humble. He is not about ego, nothing is about him."

Karina Barillas met Jim Flynn when she came to the University of Louisville on a Fullbright Scholarship in January of 1994. He had been invited to attend a reception to welcome the 13 students from Central America who had received these scholarships.

"I was leaving a difficult situation in Guatemala," Karina said. "My father had been abusive and eventually deserted our family, leaving my mother to raise me and my siblings alone. I was a good student, and I had applied for the scholarship because I was determined to make a better life for myself."

She was immediately struck by Jim's kindness and accessibility to anyone who wanted to talk with him. Having been raised in a very conservative Catholic family, priests were held in high esteem, and meeting a priest who could support her in this new venture in the United States was important.

"It meant a lot to me that he knew about Guatemala, that he had traveled there, and that he could help me in my struggles to learn English and navigate my way around life in this new country."

Karina considers Jim the founding father of the Latino Community in Kentucky, and Lupe Artiniega the founding mother. Because he spoke enough Spanish, Jim became the traveling minister at Annunciation Parish in Shelbyville where Karina was involved in forming a choir, and "encountered others who wanted to work within the Latino community in supporting and affirming other Latinos in Louisville who were struggling."

While growing up, like most women, Karina knew her place in the Catholic Church. She listened to and heeded the message: don't ask questions, don't speak out, keep your opinions to yourself. But as time went on, she gradually formed new ideas about religion and spirituality. She had experienced dire poverty in Guatemala, and she began to listen to Jim's teachings on *Liberation Theology*.

She remembers, "The more he spoke about it, the better I understood it, until finally his words caused something in my mind to click." Karina feels called on a deep level to be one with the poor. "By knowing him, liberation theology came alive for me. He accompanied me in this process of understanding it, this process of identifying with the poor and indigent. I underwent a gradual transformation."

That transformation changed Karina in significant ways.

"I began to resent the patriarchal church," she said. "I no longer believe I don't have the right to question the Church's authority. I've struggled to integrate other views of religion into my life. It's not about rules and regulations. It's much more personal than that. I know that Jesus is within me, I belong to Him and He belongs to me."

Throughout the months and years of her search, Jim became a father figure to Karina.

"I never had a father whom I could trust or who supported me," she said. "Fr. Flynn has become that father. He regards me as his daughter. In the difficult moments of my personal life, and in becoming an activist, Fr. Flynn has been there to encourage me. He is a pillar of support, offering a spirit of love and sharing. He loved me when I could not love myself."

There was a period in Karina's life when she realized she had not been to confession in a long time.

"I was mortified when I thought about it," she recalled. "I asked Fr. Flynn if he would hear my confession, and he agreed to do so. We went into a room and sat down, but he told me he had some questions for me before we began. I didn't know what was going on."

Jim began to query her, "Have you oppressed the poor? Have you exploited them? Have you taken advantage of anyone? Have you acted in a racist manner toward anyone? Have you bullied anyone?" Karina quietly answered no each time. "Well, then," he replied, and proceeded to talk about God's love.

When asked what she believes Jim's legacy will be, Karina said, "He has made the love of the Universe and the Divine accessible to everyone. He opens doors to the Divine Being of compassion and forgiveness. He broke down the stereotypes of punishment, hell and damnation for me." She compares Jim to Dorothy Day. "They are both carriers of the inspiration to identify with the poor. They are representatives of the Divine in this life. Fr. Flynn never says he's too busy to help the poor, the broken, the homeless. He is always there."

On a hot October evening in 2017, the La Casita Center presented Jim with a **Solidarity** Award. Undeterred by the heat and humidity, hundreds of people showed up to honor him. Cars lined the streets surrounding the building, and as people walked from several directions toward the Center to trudge up the steps into the hall for the meal and the award ceremony, lively music filled the air. Jim stood outside and personally greeted as many guests as he could. Once inside, people mingled, drinking, eating and laughing. Rows of long tables filled the center of the huge space, surrounded by round tables along the walls. Bright paper flowers adorned each table, and colorful garlands hung from the ceiling.

"He did not want to receive this award," Karina said. "I told him he had to do this for the community."

Mildred Menchu-Johnson, a staff person at La Casita, met Fr. Flynn in the late 1980s, during one of his trips to Guatemala.

"One of my sisters lived in the U.S., and Jim would stop by our home in Guatemala to deliver mail from her to our family," she said.

At the time, the military in Guatemala was picking up boys and young men off the city streets and in rural areas and forcing them to serve in the army. One day when Father Flynn was visiting Mildred's family in Totonicapan, one of my sisters realized our brother was missing, and she went looking for him. She asked for Father Flynn's help, and he agreed to see what he could do. Because of his intervention, Juan was released from the military.

"Fr. Flynn helped my family," Mildred said. "I remember a time when one of the generals saw him out in a rural area and offered him a ride back to Guatemala City. He did it because Fr. Flynn was white. He didn't realize that Fr. Flynn was on the side of the resistance, or he would never have done this. This was scary to us because we worried about what might happen to him if this general found out."

Jim helped Mildred get to the U.S.

"I had an illness that could possibly be treated in the United States, so he accompanied me to this country on a plane, along with my mother. And in doing so, he gave me my voice. When I arrived and settled in, he encouraged me to tell people what was really happening in Guatemala. And I did."

Jim has become a symbol of love and non-violence for Mildred. He is like an uncle to her.

"I knew I could always go to him when I needed something. In fact, he presided over my marriage. He means a lot to me. And my parents. They are still in Guatemala, and they are happy to know that there is someone in the U.S. I can turn to when I need help."

Mildred believes Jim has been "a light in the darkness for many people." She took a moment to think before adding, "Fr. Flynn offers friendship without strings attached. Many people want something in return, but he loves others because they are human, not for what they can do for him."

Maria Scharfenberger has also been a pivotal member of the group in Louisville that formed the Catholic Worker House and the La Casita Center.

"We wanted to create a lay community," she said. "We asked ourselves what a lay community might look like. We knew we wanted to use the space in service to the Latino community. The La Casita Center has become an umbrella for services to the community. We address domestic violence and provide services to women and children who often need safe places to live. We also provide broad support for Hispanic families."

According to Maria, Jim has been the "asesor" for the group. She struggled to translate the meaning of the word into its English counterpart.

"The consultant, the advisor, the mentor," she said. "And Jim is such a connector. He puts people in touch with those who help others get their ideas off the ground. You could say he is the pioneer of bringing the Hispanic ministry together."

When Maria listens to Jim preach, she says he has an unusual style of being culturally sensitive to his congregation.

"He takes into consideration the people to whom he is speaking. He speaks to injustice by using people's experiences as the springboard for teaching about faith and prayer. His homilies touch deeply on the experiences of those who are listening to him. He uses the fact that he is a gringo, and that he can say things in a way that other people wouldn't be able to. His words are simple and concise in a voice that at the same time challenges his audience. He is intimately connected to reality in his heart and mind. His words are based on the experience of the people."

Maria loves sitting down with Jim over a cup of coffee. As they converse, she learns so much within their circle of friendship and compassion. She feels cared for by him but is always learning from him and is challenged by him. He brings books and articles to share, to educate.

"But there are no judgments," she adds, "no formulas. He speaks just by being and sharing who he is."

Fr. George Kilcourse expands on this theme.

"I'm reminded of Jim every time I read Thomas Merton's elegy for Flannery O'Connor, the Catholic fiction writer from Georgia," he said. "One of

Flannery's famous sayings resonates beautifully with Jim's life and ministry. She warned us, 'Some people like their grace warm and binding, not dark and disruptive.' Only a self-absorbed bourgeois society seeks 'warm and binding' grace. The Paschal Mystery reminds Christians that the Cross is real in each of our lives. Theologian Johann Baptist Metz summons us to the 'dangerous memory' of Jesus. To risk such a danger in solidarity with the poor, the oppressed, and all the world's crucified people is to trust the God who tells us, 'I have heard the cry of my people.' Such hope, lived in solidarity, leads to the promise of a resurrected life."

It was through Maria Scharfenberger that Mary Ann and Michael Lambert first met Jim around 1994. Mary Ann recalls, "At the time, Michael and I were not involved in any type of political activity. Maria had visited St. X High School to speak to our son Brian's class about what was happening in Central America, and she told the students about an upcoming trip to Nicaragua organized by *Witness for Peace*. WFP was continuing its mission to educate Americans about the plight of Central America by arranging delegations of interested parties to travel there. When he came home from school and asked us if he could go there with a group of other students, we said yes."

Before the departure of their son, Maria called the Lamberts to thank them for allowing Brian to go. Many parents had been unwilling, fearing for their children's safety.

"We were thrilled that he wasn't afraid, and we believed he would be safe traveling with WFP members who had experience with this type of travel."

As a follow-up, when the delegation returned to the United States, Jim Flynn organized several gatherings to encourage the kids to share their experiences with other families. St. Margaret Mary Parish had also engaged some speakers to come in to discuss peace and justice issues to interested members of the congregation. During one of these meetings, Maria Scharfenberger attempted to share with those present what life was like for people living in Nicaragua, but she was greeted with negative feedback and criticism from her audience.

"Brian stood up and came to her defense," Mary Ann said. "He spoke about what he had seen and said no one should have to live like these people did. We were so proud of him."

Later Mary Ann and Michael attended a meeting at Epiphany to listen to a presentation on Central America.

"We weren't involved in any specific activities, yet," she said. "But Jim was there. And when he mentioned the need for a Secretary for the Kentucky Interfaith Task Force on Central America, I volunteered. I had been trained and worked as a secretary before, and I began assisting Jim, performing general secretarial duties for this task force."

Each year, this organization would bring at least one speaker from Latin America to provide education about what was happening, there.

"I enjoyed it very much. I was a behind-the-scenes person," Mary Ann said.

Michael, a retired engineer, was also involved in the work she was doing.

"He'd see that we got from place to place with the supplies we needed for whatever task awaited us. Michael is the kind of person who doesn't say a lot, but when he speaks, he's worth listening to."

Gradually, the work has slowed down. It became difficult to recruit new members to keep up with the range of activities that had to be done.

"Some of us old-timers can't keep up anymore," Mary Ann laughed. The task force has broadened its focus to include countries in the Caribbean. Other churches have become involved and their function is to continue helping meet the needs of migrants.

Mary Ann and Michael had wanted to visit Central America.

"But because of health issues it seems like it just never happened," she said. "But once when we were on a family vacation in the Grand Canyon, Michael and I decided we'd split from the group and at least drive down to the border. We met a friend in Tucson on our way, John Heid, who works at the border providing food and water to people trying to cross into the U.S. We had encountered him once when he came to Louisville. As we continued toward the border and began to walk around, we saw a man named Ernesto walking along the road. He had made his way from El Salvador, leaving with five other guys, though he was now alone. John provided this man much-needed food and water and determined that his condition required a visit to a near-by clinic. He told us to continue walking and he'd catch up with us later. We were immensely touched by this experience. It was a beautiful moment in our lives, and we felt like Christ was present in this encounter."

Michael Lambert referred to Jim's writings.

"Jim is a prolific writer," he said, "and his writings have affected me. I've read a lot of what he has written in letters to the editor and other places," he said. "I remember one letter in the *Louisville Courier Journal* about some African-American kids in the west end who had gotten in serious trouble, causing criticism of them to pour in from all sides. But Jim came to their defense. He looks more deeply into issues because he understands that extenuating circumstances, such as poverty and racism, can come into play in these situations. And some of his homilies have been learning experiences for me. If he says something about Scripture, and he contradicts one of the bishops, I'm going with Jim."

Mary Ann and Michael are grateful that Jim has become a role model for their son and daughter-in-law.

"Jim is the most dedicated, Christ-like person I've ever met," Mary Ann said. "He is compassionate and genuine. There is nothing phony about him. He becomes angry over the mistreatment of others. He's just a wonderful man, and I am so thankful we have had the opportunity to work with him. He is a dear friend."

John Burke adds, "My consciousness has been opened up by Jim, but no matter how much my thinking has evolved, Jim is always at least three steps ahead of me. He learned Spanish when he was 55, so he could become fluent enough to understand what was happening in Central America."

In the early 90s, John traveled to El Salvador and Guatemala on a retreat to honor the priests and nuns who were victims of the violence that had occurred there.

"As I moved around these countries, whenever I'd mention to people that I knew Jim Flynn, I quickly realized that everyone knew him."

John has no doubt that Jim's legacy will be a lasting one.

"My friendship with Jim has been of utmost importance to me. He is a friend who has a vision of a more just world, and who did all he could to make that a reality. He has fought the good fight, kept the faith, and kept hope alive."

John quoted Micah, 6:8 "'Act justly, love tenderly, walk humbly with your God.' Jim has done those things. I am so grateful for his friendship. Jim may be a little guy, but he has huge shoes to fill."

Pope Francis's teachings to the world, according to John, "certify Jim's beliefs about service to the poor, to the people on the margins of society, and that these beliefs are not tangential to Christianity."

David Horvath hates to think of doing social justice work without Jim.

"His absence will leave a big hole," he said. "I will have lost a personal friend who is near and dear to me. The world will have lost another prophet. He is a constant, loving reminder that we are all interconnected on this planet and in this universe, and that we have a specific responsibility to those on the margins to whom we owe our solidarity. In his political justice work, he is so good at sowing seeds and nurturing tender plants."

Pat Geier remains close friends with Jim.

"We share a long history and many mutual interests. We've done a lot of hiking, cycling, and skiing together. We share a love of classical music. We are both avid readers and devotees of John Dominic Crossan, Thomas Berry and Diarmuid O'Murchu. Jim's always a half-a-dozen books ahead of me. He's a life-long learner, something I greatly admire about him. He has always had a great openness to the future."

Pat teared up when asked what Jim means to her, the community-at-large, and the Church. She paused for a moment before responding.

"I don't generally have Scripture verses pop into my head," she said. "But these words come to mind. It's the passage in the Gospels, Jesus's inaugural address . . . 'The Spirit of the Lord is upon me . . . to bring glad tidings to the poor . . .' This sums up Jim's life. And it has come at a price. He's had his share of rejection from the powers that be, both religious and civil, and remains somewhat ostracized. He comforts the afflicted and afflicts the comfortable—the latter being most of us. At the same time, he has a great tenderness for people, especially those who've had the boot on their necks."

Pat drew a distinction between Jim's pastoral capabilities and his prophetic voice.

"He will not go down in history as a conventional pastor," she said. "His prophetic voice will be his legacy. His gift is to be out in the streets, being the voice of those without a voice. Like the prophets in the Old Testament, he is an outsider in many ways—he usually doesn't back off from challenging civil and, at times, religious authority."

How does Jim escape arrogance and self-righteousness? According to Pat, "He has plenty of righteousness, but it's not personal, it's not about him. He feels deeply about injustice. He's a fighter. He comes from Irish immigrants and he's never forgotten his history. But he's also quite humble. You can see that in his lifestyle, in his generosity, in his close relationships with poor people and immigrants." Pat thought further about her answer before adding, "Sometimes he can be so far out in front that he becomes impatient with those who are not quite where he is. When he believes a cause is just, it's difficult at times for him to tolerate the apathy and intransigence of others."

For Pat, the loss of Jim Flynn would be, "An unspeakable sorrow. He has given me more than I can express. How does one say 'thank you' for such a gift? I think it's about paying it forward."

Barbara Aubrey concurs.

"I will probably outlive him," she said. "I don't like to even think about that. What will we do without him? His legacy will be to keep doing what he taught us to do. He lives every word that comes out of his mouth. He is a prophet and a visionary who sees what is to come before others do. What I want people to know about him, what I want to tell everyone is that he is one of the most Christ-like people I've ever known, and I am blessed he has been part of my life."

In a further tribute to Jim, George Kilcourse again calls on Thomas Merton.

"Like Merton voiced in his elegy for O'Connor, I write Jim's name with 'honor'—for all he has taught us, for all that he has witnessed and shared through his ongoing conversion experience, for his embrace of the 'dangerous memory' of Jesus."

Some of Jim's family eventually shifted their views toward his. Ed points out, "Because Jim is a leader, he challenged our habitual ways of thinking. He's not a charge-up-the-hill kind of leader. He makes you think.

And he doesn't chicken out as many of us sometimes do. He doesn't. He stands his ground."

"Jim definitely marches to the beat of a different drummer," he stated. "I admire his courage and persistence. It takes a lot of guts to keep saying what you believe when it goes against the majority opinion. Mom and Dad lived long enough to be indescribably proud of him." Then he laughed and added, "But Jim is a man of contradictions, too. We used to tease him when he'd take trips to the mountains to ski. Here he is, a man always concerned about the poor, skiing in Utah. While he was out there, he met the CEO of Deer Valley, one of the ski areas, and suggested that he purchase fair trade coffee for their guests."

Jim said later, "I also met the CEO of the Sundance ski area and brought up the idea of fair trade coffee. He agreed to do the same. I don't know if they still purchase it, but they did back then."

In 2002, Jim traveled with some family members to Ireland, hoping to satisfy their curiosity about their Irish ancestry.

"We wanted to trace our roots," Jim said. "We wanted to return to our roots, to discover why our ancestors left Ireland. Despite our efforts, we could only find information that led us to County Cork."

But while in Ireland, an opportunity occurred that is not always available to visitors. Ed discovered that weather conditions might be conducive to making a trip to Skellig Michael, a large rock that juts out of the ocean where ancient monks had established a monastery centuries ago. Today, it is set aside as a World UNESCO Heritage Site.

"A boat transports you to the spot where you can step onto the island, but if the current is too choppy, it is not safe to disembark," Jim said. "But the day we went, the water was calm enough to allow us to jump out onto the rocks and climb the hundreds of steps carved from the bare stone all the way to the top. We had brought our lunch," Jim remembered, "but we didn't realize parts of the island are off-limits to the public. When we sat down and began to eat, a gentleman told us we'd have to move to another section. As we resettled on a rock and looked around, it's pretty much the way it was back in the 6th century, windswept and cold, and when you look down, it is straight down. We saw the stone huts where the monks lived, and it's impossible to figure out what they ate, or how they eked out a living. It was a sobering and wonderful experience."

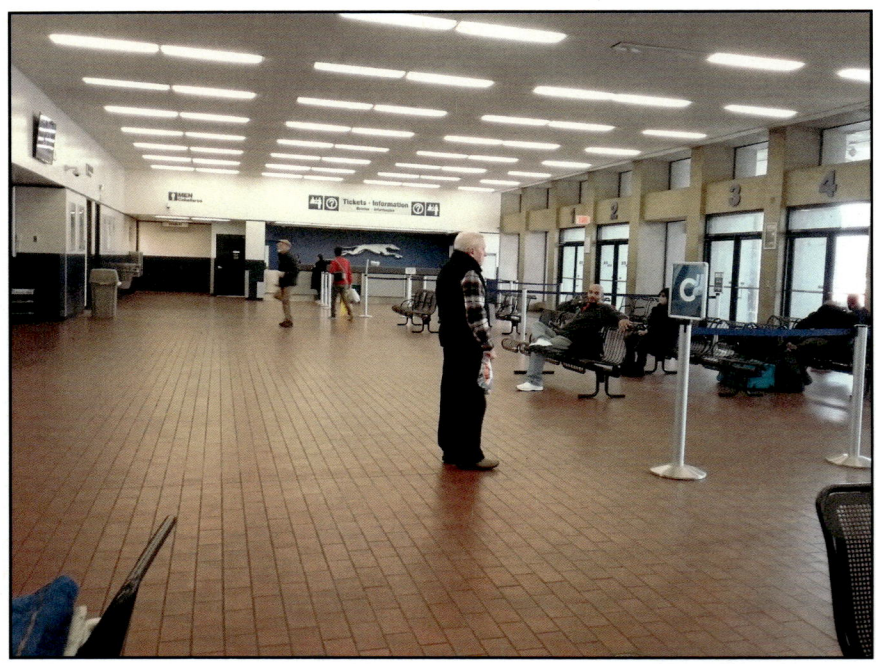

*Jim Flynn waits daily with others to greet immigrants
and pass out needed supplies at the Greyhound bus station in downtown Louisville.*

CHAPTER 11

Immigration has long been a thorny and divisive issue in the United States. Many who arrived here from other shores to make better lives for themselves became possessive about their new country, and early on discrimination against immigrants began to weave itself into the warp and weft of American history. The debate has taken one of its ugliest turns in the summer of 2018. President Trump's administration is separating children from their parents as they cross into the U.S. as part of his "zero tolerance policy" toward people trying to cross our southern border. Not only has the removal of the children been horrific and devastating, it has aroused the ire of American citizens across the country, even some who had previously supported President Trump. It quickly became clear that this administration had no plans in place to return these children to their parents, many of whom are being housed in tent-cities and detention centers whose locations are being kept secret.

Jim wrote a response to these horrendous policies on the part of the U.S. government called, 'A STORY.' It reads in part, "And so it came to pass. A ruler in Egypt ordered his top attorney to demand that border guards stop desperate peoples trying to cross into Egypt. The King knew that parents with children were fleeing massacres in their homelands, but Egypt would not accommodate hordes of refugees, with fears that some could be intent on bringing harm to citizens of Egypt. The Egyptian ruler and his attorney seemed to be on a campaign to demonize and criminalize those migrants seeking refuge. . . So, the call went out to the border agents to separate children from parents if they tried to cross the border . . . Mothers may wail in uncontrollable moans, but the message must go out to one and all back where the massacres around Bethlehem raged: 'if you try this tactic we will snatch your child and imprison you parents . . . we have a 'zero tolerance' in place to discourage immigration. . .'" After continuing the story, comparing turning away immigrants with turning away Joseph and Mary at the time of Jesus' birth, Jim ends with a quote from the Book of Hebrews: "Do not neglect to show hospitality to strangers, for by this some have entertained angels without knowing it" (Heb. 13:2).

To millions of people, this is one of the lowest points in our history. In the November 17, 2017 issue of *The Atlantic* on page 19, Yoni Applebaum writes: "Americans have been most successful when fighting over how to draw closer to the promise of their democracy; how to fulfill their threefold commitment to equality, rights and opportunity; and how to distribute the resulting prosperity. They have been held together by the conviction that the United States had a unique mission, even as they debated how to pursue it." Citizens like Rev. James Flynn have helped keep the debate alive by tirelessly calling on us to keep the promises of our democracy and devoting himself to social justice and the pursuit of equality for all.

Continuing, Yoni Applebaum cautions: "The greatest danger facing American democracy is complacence. The democratic experiment is fragile, and its continued survival improbable. Salvaging it will require enlarging opportunity, restoring rights, and pursuing equality, and thereby renewing faith in the system that delivers them. This, really, is the American idea: that prosperity and justice do not exist in tension, but flow from each other. Achieving that ideal will require fighting as if the fate of democracy itself rests upon the struggle— because it does."

Dianne Aprile, a former *Louisville Courier Journal* reporter and local author knows Jim personally. He was the assistant pastor of the Catholic parish where she grew up. She wrote an article in the December 21, 1997 issue of the paper, reflecting a conversation she had with Jim, which prompted her to raise these questions.

When and where did we in the United States lose our welcoming spirit? Do lawmakers in our Congress really speak for us? How do they look into the creche sets under their Christmas trees or in their friends' homes and not make the connection? As the Christmas story unfolds each year, don't we assure ourselves we would never have closed our inns to Jesus, Mary and Joseph? But today it is Jose, Maria and Raquel knocking at the door. And the inn they have come to is not in faraway Bethlehem, but right here in our own back yard.

Attitudes toward immigrants haven't changed much since 1997, when Dianne Aprile raised these questions. It's people like Jim who keep asking them.

Twenty-one years later, in the Thursday, June 21, 2018 issue of the *Louisville Courier Journal*, reporter Joseph Gerth writes

Every day except Sundays for the past five months, the Rev. Jim Flynn has stood on a street corner for one hour, preaching the Gospel in just four words: **'Immigrants and Refugees Welcome.'** It's a message especially compelling now as our nation has separated children from their parents who cross into this country without permission and told victims of domestic violence and gang violence that they can't seek asylum here. To date, more than 2,300 children who illegally crossed the border with adults have been separated from their parents.

Further in the article, Mr. Gerth quotes Jim: "I feel like there is fascism emerging," said Flynn, who for decades has fought for social justice, particularly as it relates to American involvement in South and Central America. "It's racism and xenophobia and it's being fanned from the top." The article ends with Jim's chilling words: "I look around and I see Germany in the 1930s right now," he said. "I'm scared."

On Saturday, June 30, 2018, hundreds of thousands of people gathered in cities across the United States to protest Trump's zero-tolerance policy towards immigrants. On this blistering hot day, in the midst of the huge crowd that stood on the steps and poured out into the street in front of Metro Hall in downtown Louisville, Jim Flynn sat on a concrete wall behind the large banner that accompanies him to many events: **Immigrants and Refugees Welcome**. Four powerful words. No showboating. No shouting. No parading back and forth. No drawing attention to himself. No self-aggrandizing. No fist pumping. Just his persistent, resistant presence that has drawn attention for so many years to the fact that it is not okay to discriminate against anyone, that justice is due to all human beings, from the least powerful to the mightiest, and that we are all a part of shared humanity.

Recently, PBS broadcast a series of shows called, *Poetry in America*. Each show highlighted a discussion of one poem from the perspective of several different people. On the July 17, 2018 program, the chosen poem was, *The New Colossus*, by Emma Lazarus. Those interviewed by Elise New, the moderator, were children or grandchildren of immigrants from Ecuador, Russia, and Vietnam. Most of us would probably not have recognized this poem when the title was announced until we heard several of its most famous lines. Here is the poem in its entirety:

THE NEW COLOSSUS

Not like the brazen giant of Greek fame,
With conquering limbs astride from land to land;
Here at our sea-washed sunset gates shall stand
A mighty woman with a torch, whose flame
Is the imprisoned lightning; and her name
Mother of Exiles. From her beacon-hand
Glows world-wide welcome; and her mild eyes command
The air-bridged harbor that twin cities frame.
"Keep ancient lands, your storied pomp!" cries she
With silent lips. "Give me your tired, your poor,
Your huddled masses yearning to breathe free,
The wretched refuse of your teeming shore.
Send these, the homeless, tempest-tost to me,
I lift my lamp beside the golden door.

During one moment of the show, pre-recorded news footage of a pro-immigration rally was shown that had taken place somewhere in the United

States, highlighting signs held by some of the marchers with images of the Statue of Liberty and messages for immigrants: **SHE STANDS FOR YOU; WE STAND FOR YOU; REFUGEES WELCOME**.

Another PBS show that aired during the summer of 2018, called, *No Passport Required,* found Chef Marcus Samuelsson, himself an immigrant born in Ethiopia and raised in Sweden before moving to the United States, traveling around the country, exploring the remarkable contributions immigrants have made to the United States. Two points made during this show run counter to what many Americans persist in believing about people who come to this country seeking better lives, as they flee from poverty, violence, and terror. The first point is that immigrants do not take jobs away from those who are already here. The real story is they open hundreds of small businesses that create jobs for many people. They also work at jobs that many Americans refuse to do. The second point is that independent studies have shown that crime rates go down in areas where immigrants live in large numbers, despite the intense efforts of fear-mongers to claim that all immigrants who come to this country are criminals.

In the August 23, 2018 edition of the *Louisville Courier Journal,* in an article reprinted from *The Des Moines Register,* we read: "NO . . . immigrants don't commit more crimes than US-born people." In a quote by Walter Ewing, a Senior Researcher at the American Immigration Council, we read: "There's 100 years of data from all different sources that all point in the same direction. If you don't believe one study, there's 10 more behind it that say the same thing." And further:

Missing from that discussion was any proof that immigrants are more likely to commit crimes or acts of terrorism than native-born Americans. Immigration experts, including academic researchers, have said that's because all available national crime statistics show immigrants commit fewer crimes, not more, than those born in the U.S. Even opponents of increased immigration lack evidence linking immigrants to higher crime rates.

Add one more voice to the mix. In the August 20, 2018 edition of the *Louisville Courier Journal,* guest columnist, Jeffrey Roth, the Deputy Commissioner of the New York City Department of Veterans' Services, wrote:

While this country may be deeply divided on issues involving immigration, naturalization through military service is an excellent means for capable, competent and honorable people to become citizens. They do a service to our country while they wear the uniform, and we as a nation reap the benefits of their experience once they've completed their tours. We should consider ourselves fortunate to have any and all who've served join the ranks of our citizenry. And our country will be stronger for it.

Jim tells a story that he heard from one of the women in the planning group he met with regularly during one of their strategizing sessions.

"It seems that two new attorneys have recently been hired in Louisville to defend immigrants, and they happen to be Native Americans," he said. "Since they are descendants of the First People in this country, they have facetiously raised the issue of whether they will need to work on deporting all people who are not indigenous to the Americas." He laughed quietly, then added, "Many people forget that, with the exception of Native Americans, and the African-Americans who were forced to come here, we are all immigrants."

The Rev. James Flynn prefers not to talk about himself. Ask him what he thinks, what he believes, or what he feels, and he will respond by describing what he has done. The Gospel of St. Matthew says, "By their deeds you shall know them." In the *Upajjhatthana Sutta* the Buddha says, "My deeds are the ground on which I stand." The Koran teaches that it is good deeds that will help a person into Paradise.

If deeds provide the measure of a person, it would be difficult to overstate how solid the ground is upon which Jim Flynn has stood for most of his life, and upon which he continues to stand.

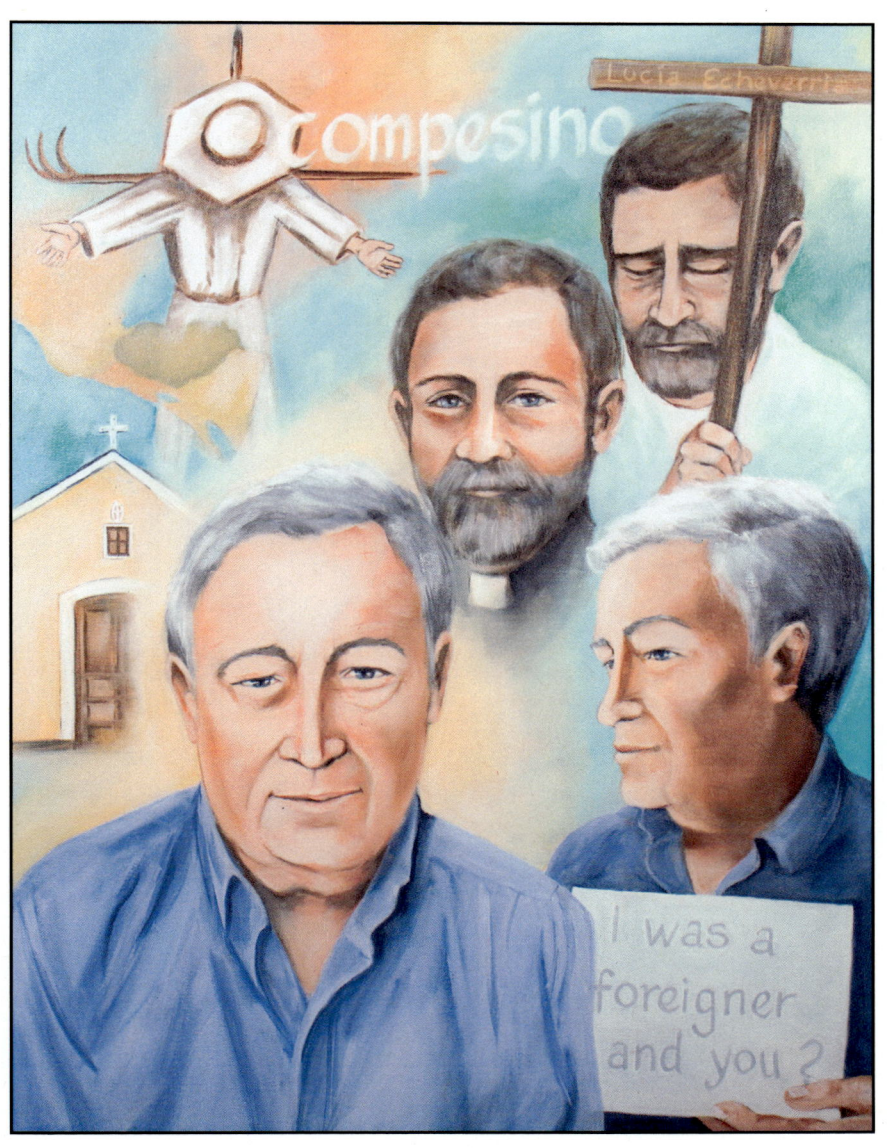

Original Oil Painting by Joan Zehnder

Additional Referenced Materials

No One's Easy Daughter: Our Journeys of Transformation. Mary H. Ber, Sue Koeppel, Mary Colgan McNamara, OSF (Eds), 2017. ImagoPress: Tuscon, AZ.

Solnit, Rebecca. *Hope in the Dark*. Haymarket Books: Chicago, IL.

ACKNOWLEDGEMENTS

I would like to thank each person who sat for an interview to share his or her memories of and experiences with Jim. Not only did they give the time required for the interview, each of them then took the transcribed interview and made it their own by correcting any mistakes or misperceptions on my part. They also added to the richness of each interview by polishing it to more deeply reflect their personal connections to Jim. This book could not have been written without them.